Other Books by Ernest J. Zarra III

Assaulted: Violence in Schools and What Needs to Be Done, 2018

The Teacher Exodus: Reversing the Trend and Keeping Teachers in Classrooms, 2018

The Entitled Generation: Helping Teachers Teach and Reach the Minds and Hearts of Generation Z, 2017

Helping Parents Understand the Minds and Hearts of Generation Z, 2017

Common Sense Education: From Common Core to ESSA and Beyond, 2016

The Wrong Direction for Today's Schools: The Impact of Common Core on American Education, 2015

Teacher-Student Relationships: Crossing Into the Emotional, Physical, and Sexual Realms, 2013

The Age of Teacher Shortages

The Age of Teacher Shortages

Reasons, Responsibilities, Reactions

Ernest J. Zarra III

ROWMAN & LITTLEFIELD
Lanham • Boulder • New York • London

Published by Rowman & Littlefield
An imprint of The Rowman & Littlefield Publishing Group, Inc.
4501 Forbes Boulevard, Suite 200, Lanham, Maryland 20706
www.rowman.com

6 Tinworth Street, London SE11 5AL

Copyright © 2019 by Ernest J. Zarra III

All rights reserved. No part of this book may be reproduced in any form or by any electronic or mechanical means, including information storage and retrieval systems, without written permission from the publisher, except by a reviewer who may quote passages in a review.

British Library Cataloguing in Publication Information Available

Library of Congress Cataloging-in-Publication Data

Names: Zarra, Ernest J., 1955– author.
Title: The age of teacher shortages : reasons, responsibilities, reactions / Ernest J. Zarra, III.
Description: Lanham : Rowman & Littlefield, [2019] | Includes bibliographical references and index.
 | Summary: "The Age of Teacher Shortages is a practical look at the reasons for teacher shortages in schools across America, and suggests solutions"—Provided by publisher.
Identifiers: LCCN 2019016326 (print) | LCCN 2019981492 (ebook) | ISBN 9781475850048 (cloth) | ISBN 9781475850055 (pbk.) | ISBN 9781475850062 (ebook)
Subjects: LCSH: Teachers—Supply and demand—United States. | Teacher turnover—United States—Prevention.
Classification: LCC LB2833.2 .Z36 2019 (print) | LCC LB2833.2 (ebook) | DDC 371.1—dc23
LC record available at https://lccn.loc.gov/2019016326
LC ebook record available at https://lccn.loc.gov/2019981492

This book is dedicated to my first grandchild . . . Max.
This book was conceived when you were born.
The Almighty knew just what was needed to prompt this project.
I will always love you!

Contents

List of Tables	xi
Preface	xiii
Acknowledgments	xix
1 Cultural Changes Affecting American Public Education	1
2 Vanishing Passion	27
3 Incentivizing Mediocrity	51
4 Teaching—Perception versus Reality	77
5 Attracting and Retaining Teachers	101
Appendix A: Teacher Vacancies and Uncertified/Noncredentialed Teachers	125
Appendix B: Select Sample of State-Level Alternative Pathways to Certification (APCs)	143
Index	149
About the Author	155

List of Tables

Table 2.1	High school student interest in pursuing education as a major in college	38
Table 2.2	Incoming college freshmen students expressing interest in teaching	39
Table 2.3	College students enrolled in teacher education programs	40
Table 3.1	US states and territories with teacher shortages by category, 2017–2018	54
Table 3.2	Select states with induction and mentoring requirements	57

Preface

As a result of a job change, many miles and hours have been logged on airplanes. The privilege of being on board flights predominantly comprised of college students enables some very interesting informal conversations. In preparation for this book, it was my aim to engage in conversations with many captive window-seated university students. On every flight I take out of a college-town airport, I ask a few simple questions meant as icebreakers. My intention is to listen carefully to their responses and then attempt to delve into a couple of additional follow-up questions. These questions are intentional conversational shifts toward careers in education, or their experiences as students throughout their K–12 schooling.

The deliberate questions asked included "What is your major?" and "Would you consider teaching in public schools? Why or why not?" The replies to these questions enable a shift in the conversation, which always seems to come down to three areas: (1) economics, (2) opportunities for women to train for employment in STEAM (science, technology, engineering, art, and mathematics) areas, and (3) reasons for general disenchantment with certain K–12 experiences students had in their own schooling. This last response always speaks volumes.

Interestingly enough, some of the young people who continued conversations were quick to add either that their parents were teachers and pressed their children to pursue different careers or that the indictment on their own generation was that today's students are so entitled and far too soft. Essentially, Generation Z was critiquing itself thirty-five thousand feet in the sky, and it was discovering it did not enjoy many of its own personal schooling experiences.

Well, if our schools and the current generation of students and parents are not the evangelists to attract a new generation of teachers, the nation is in trouble. Add to this inability the annual exodus of current education *good news advocates*—namely, thousands of public school teachers. Hence, the terms *education* and *excellence* are quickly being divorced from mention in the same breath.

The problems appear too large to solve, the efforts too small to do anything more than attempt to stop states' hemorrhaging of classroom teachers. Why do Americans tolerate rhetoric about public education that points to an unrealistic message?

REASONS FOR WRITING THIS BOOK

Traditional training of teachers from teacher training institutions is undergoing major revisions. Not only are the on-campus, face-to-face programs being revised, but also entirely new pathways have been devised to accommodate the entry of newer teachers. States are also changing the requirements to obtain initial credentials, in order to fill slots in districts across their states. The first reason for writing this book is to detail the shifts in American culture that have contributed to a loss of interest by college students to enter the fields of education and teacher training.

Second, after laying out these cultural changes, this book then examines the consequences of these changes and the responses by states and districts. The reality is that with this new age of teacher shortages, and the subsequent policy and programmatic changes realized at state and district levels, there is a mad dash to place teachers in classrooms as quickly as possible. For example, people are being granted state-level credentials that allow them to teach in classrooms with the title, but without the teacher training to which Americans have become accustomed.

The third reason for writing this book is to address mentoring and professional development of new teachers. Based on research of current and trending educational needs, this book clearly lays out the need for professional development in tandem with the high demand for new and untrained teachers. Some of these newer teachers are coming by way of second-career choices, and more and more are bypassing the traditional routes to the classroom. This makes professional development all the more important.

A fourth reason for writing this book is to examine why Gen Z has little passion for choosing to spend a career in teaching in public schools. Along with this lack of passion, the book also investigates the reasons so many veteran teachers are walking away from storied and impacting careers before their time.

One additional reason for writing this book is to explore and critique some of the various pathway possibilities available to those seeking to enter teaching from nontraditional routes. Alternative certifications are becoming more and more acceptable by states and local school districts. What are the benefits and costs to second-career teachers who choose their training outside the traditional pathways? Also explored are some of the unintended consequences that affect students and their families.

EXPEDIENCY OVER SUFFICIENCY

Sometimes policymakers create their own problems without thinking through the unintended consequences of their actions. It is as if there are competing value structures at work, especially when it comes to education issues. Politicians and bureaucrats see issues and budgets. Teachers see children and relationships.

Those making decisions that affect children and relationships are caught between what is today a massive problem of teacher shortages. No one can fault them for acting with what they would consider the most expedient fashion to meet the staffing needs in districts in their states.

Teachers view the shortages for a variety of reasons and are in a bind as well. Do they stand as one and support their state and districts that are placing untrained people in rooms next door to them, or do they lobby for what is sufficient to the training they received, knowing full well that students are shortchanged with anything less? This comes down to politicians acting on expediency on behalf of teachers requesting sufficiency. This disparity is responsible for part of the teacher shortage, as some teachers leave the classrooms early because of the disparity.

A very tangible reason that teachers are concerned about expedient actions of the states and districts is the allowance to train teachers online. Some have expressed concern that teachers trained online, although being allowed to fill open teaching positions in the process, will wind up shortchanged for the very jobs for which they have been hired.

Online training is being criticized for the way it is presented because it is not preparing potential teachers for the real world they will face. Yet, when the philosophy of the program is to fill the needs created by shortages, then expediency over sufficiency is the fundamental rationale for colleges to offer these programs.

INSPIRATION FOR THE BOOK

With the completion of four decades of educational experience, it is a foregone conclusion that students were the inspiration for this book. Indeed, students are my first source of inspiration for this book. Over the years I have been influenced by tens of thousands of students and their families, and the affects between us have been exponential. While this is true, I also credit the birth of a grandchild as another level of inspiration—one that is deeply soulful on a familial level and surpasses the professional.

There is something about holding a new life and speculating the what-ifs of his or her future. There is also the concern of what schools will be like for the newborn child in just a few short years once schooling begins. That being said, I am also deeply inspired by those teachers-in-training at the moment, and their futures as well, as they affect the lives of children and young adults in their classrooms. Some of these in training are my mentees.

If all teacher education departments were as fortunate as I am to have such awesome teacher candidates who are deeply trained in the relevant and the practical as they are in the professional, the world of American public education would be a much better place. The next generation of teachers certainly has an advocate in me, a new grandfather, former classroom teacher, and current college professor of teacher education.

STRUCTURE OF THE BOOK

The structure of this book is configured so that the reader will be presented with an understanding of some of the cultural changes that have occurred in the United States, each of which have their affects upon public schools and children. These changes in culture have affected the supply of new teachers in the teacher education pipeline, the struggle for replacing early retirees, the disenchanted, and those simply making other career choices. These challenges, combined with others, have placed states in desperation mode.

This desperation has led states to devise alternative plans for teacher certification, as a strategy to ease the pathways to the classrooms and alleviate the desperation felt, in terms of teacher shortages. In addition to the cultural changes that have led some to leave teaching, this book also explores the opportunities available as incentives for people to join the teaching ranks through both traditional and nontraditional avenues.

Chapter 1 presents the case for American culture affecting public education and, through some of these effects, how the culture has been partly responsible for teacher shortages in the nation. The concerns of mandates and programs and the focus on marginalized groups for the sake of equity have driven wedges into the unity of schools and classrooms. Teachers no longer sense they have any autonomy over decision-making in the areas of classroom management and discipline and curriculum.

Chapter 2 analyzes why there is vanishing passion among teachers in general, those considering other careers over teaching, and the veterans willing to walk away from their jobs in public schools. Chapter 3 explores the notion that American public schools are settling for less than good education, as they aspire to mediocrity, while claiming to hold students and teachers to higher standards. The contrast between expediency over sufficiency addresses choices made in desperation and the costs and benefits of such choices.

Chapter 4 digs into the perceptions of education that are meant to attract teachers by verbal or programmatic incentives, enticing them into the classrooms. Contrasted are the ways some of these perceptions are in conflict with the realities faced by teachers and their experiences. The presentation of perspectives of teaching by real teachers will inform the reader as to what teaching is like in American public schools. The intention is for teachers to choose to enter a career based on reality and to be hired with their eyes wide open, instead of false notions predicated on idealism.

Chapter 5 details some of the strategies employed by states and districts, in order to attract and retain teachers in districts. Induction programs and mentoring are addressed, as well as suggested professional development academies. Districts must tackle the lack of teacher education and training, so that teachers coming into classrooms by nontraditional teacher education programs have a good chance of career longevity.

There are two very important and helpful appendixes at the back of the book for those seeking employment and those seeking to become teachers through an Alternative Pathway to Certification (APC). Appendix A is a tool for the reader to be able to compare locations of recent teacher shortages and openings for those seeking employment within the United States. Data from the Learning Policy Institute and elsewhere have been assembled to provide a bird's-eye view to those wishing to enter teaching in American public schools.

Appendix B is a select sample of several states and includes ways to pursue alternative certification via nontraditional pathways. The types of certifications and many of the requirements for licensure along those pathways are listed for the reader, according to the sample states' documents.

Acknowledgments

Acknowledgments are sometimes hard to put to paper. An author does not want to leave anyone out of the equation, in terms of support—not only for the book but also for affecting life and career. So, to begin, I am reminded of the genesis of this book. This book came on the heels of a previous book, *The Teacher Exodus: Reversing the Trend and Keeping Teachers in the Classrooms.*

I extended the research because there continued a mass exodus of teachers from their careers, and many of these teachers were just leaving for other employment. The mass exodus has now moved the nation's public schools into what I refer to as the *musical chair mode.*

Reminiscent of the game musical chairs, *The Age of Teacher Shortages: Reasons, Responsibilities, Reactions* is being played out in American schools. The music is playing, and there are plenty of chairs, because only a few teachers remain. There is less competition for jobs. Rather than more teachers than chairs, the reverse is true. There is no longer a game being played out. Still teachers remain!

I acknowledge those teachers who remain in the game and face the music, knowing that their job is becoming more and more difficult with each passing year. We are no longer in a teacher shortage condition; we are now in an *Age of Teacher Shortages*—and these shortages are throughout the entire system and touch every state, and almost every level from kindergarten through twelfth grade.

Fortunately, I had the privilege of teaching thousands of students throughout my career as a public and private school teacher. I would be remiss if I did not acknowledge the affects of these students and their families in my life. On the flip side, I also acknowledge my own former teachers with whom, incidentally, I have the honor of sharing the same decade.

Many thanks go out to the readers and reviewers of my work, and my collegial partners in teacher education at Lewis-Clark State College. Your feedback and professional insights are so very much appreciated. I am deeply indebted to my teacher education students at the college. They have embraced me as a professor, in grace and with patience—and they listened and helped refine many substantive points along the way.

I acknowledge once again Suzi, my wife and lifelong partner. Her experience as an educator, and a highly intuitive idea critic, has served to correct and improve my sometimes-rambling thoughts. Two educators in a family is a blessing, though sometimes our children did not think so.

Finally, I want to acknowledge the fictitious musicians who still play the musical chairs tunes all over the nation, even as the number of teacher-players continues to diminish. Play on, but don't rearrange the chairs just yet.

Chapter One

Cultural Changes Affecting American Public Education

> The task of the modern educator is not to cut down jungles but to irrigate deserts. The right defence against false sentiments is to inculcate just sentiments. By starving the sensibility of our pupils we only make them easier prey to the propagandist when he comes.[1]

As Generation Z attends school, graduates from college, and shares the workplace with other generations, this sharing presents several cultural challenges. Yet, such challenges are not unusual. Gen Z's transition has had its share of challenges as it adjusts. Its continued transition brings with it certain dispositions, enhanced by their propensity to rely on technology for most of their daily regimen of work and leisure.

Gen Z are tech-dependent and generally do not know a time before the internet and smart devices. In terms of access to technology and many uses for devices, their "unlimited and constant connection to the internet fosters major challenges for Gen Z. . . . They also constantly face an overflow of information from all kinds of sources that makes it hard for them to analyze, discriminate and trust. This generation lives immersed in a web of divergent ideas and morality without the necessary time and maturity to reflect about them and respond appropriately."[2] In the words of C. S. Lewis, "when poisons become fashionable, they do not cease to kill."[3] Fashionability does not circumvent effect. Is the very technology that has produced a new generation of addicts the ultimate cultural arsenic?

GENERATIONAL CHANGE

The cultural shift attributed to a generation affects not only mindsets and beliefs but also priorities and practices. In terms of worldviews about values and faith, Gen Z must be viewed through the lens that focuses on the fact that its members "were born in a context where religion in general, and Christianity in particular, are no longer a major influence in American culture. The secularization of society has been a trend in the last few years, especially in the western world, and Gen Z are growing up in this new social context . . . teens 13–18 are twice as likely as adults to say they are atheists."[4] This is quite a change from a generation ago, which experienced the Jesus Movement and the explosion of competing Eastern religions upon society.

That being the case, in some ways Gen Z are more secular compared to previous generations. They celebrate the fact that they affirm open-mindedness and sensitivities "to other people's feelings and opinions."[5] Likewise, "they embrace divergent perspectives and are more inclusive than previous generations. They are comfortable with people who are different than them and tend to be less judgmental because of those differences."[6] But are these changes cultural contradictions or exhibitions of cultural confluence?

Contradiction and Confusion

As a result of their belief that judging others' motives is wrong, they apply personal hypocrisy and judgmental spirit toward those expressing any traditional moral view, or the espousal of a traditional set of beliefs or practices that counter their own. Therefore, judging others as wrong by their openness not to judge others is a badge of contradiction that Gen Z is apparently willing to wear.

Furthermore, Gen Z are set apart from other generations by their "flexible moral compass that leads them to unclear paths and prevents them from making decisions or judgments according to solid values and convictions."[7] Technology and easy access to information supportive of their views, whether valid or not, emboldens their confidence. After all, an online world that offers a smorgasbord of support for one's personal biases is most affirming and immediately gratifying. There is strength in numbers, and Gen Z is definitely a participant in groupthink.

An example of groupthink is seen in turning away from traditional morality. This is best viewed in the shift toward accepting gender fluidity. Gen Z tend to feel that "gender is how a person feels inside and not the birth sex"[8] that parents, doctors, or biology lay claim. In fact, "Gen Z may have a tendency to express evolving views about their sexuality because of a great desire to empathize with marginalized groups. They tend to express solidarity with people with different perspectives about gender issues,"[9] which, again, is an example of their rejection of tradition in favor of a more secular, pop humanity and identity.

In a display of added confusion, Gen Z sometimes views the family from a traditional perspective. However, they characteristically stop short in allowing family to thrust the expectation of identity upon them. Interestingly enough, "parents are the most important people and the greatest influence for children. . . . Gen Z admire their parents, but at the same time they don't feel family relationships are central to their sense of self. They love their parents, but . . . this generation is suffering the consequences of many broken families and distant parents who lack the time, resources or energy to raise them."[10] Although there are many differences found between Gen Z and other generations, there are two interesting commonalities between them.

Generational Commonality

The first commonality is their perspective on materialism and the accumulation of goods. These do not seem to have been sacrificed with the emergence of Gen Z. In fact, given our nation's predisposition to materialism and money, the culture of Gen Z "tends to measure success in financial terms . . . shadowing these ideals with even more enthusiasm than previous generations."[11] The second commonality is Gen Z's strident and unrelenting emphasis on racial reconciliation. Although racial tensions still appear from time to time in our society, "Gen Z can become agents of reconciliation for the church and society as a whole."[12] However, both Gen Z and institutions of faith must reconcile their positions on gender and twenty-first-century expressions of sexuality. That being said, there is a glimmer of hope on the horizon. As with most generations, maturity speaks volumes about changes in personal and group perspectives. So, time will tell.

CHANGES IN STUDENTS' THINKING

Neuroscientists inform us that students' brains are wiring up very differently in twenty-first-century American children.[13] They believe that due to the affect of screen time, and the uses of devices that earmark addiction, students have become less receptive to laying down their devices throughout seven-hour school days. As a result, the research indicates that prolonged use of smart devices is affecting their moods and motivation.[14] As teachers can attest, there have been changes in the ways of thinking among Gen Z. Teachers battle regularly over the use of smartphones, and there are anecdotes aplenty that enable people to draw their own conclusions.

Students have access to more information, but the depth of this access is sometimes sacrificed by the distractions of attraction, caused by the uses of devices in the lives of students. Changing brains lead to changing beliefs and ideas. Is it any wonder that Gen Z has become promoters of ideas once thought untenable just a few years ago? Changes in ideas lead to changes in moral practices, faith beliefs, ideas about gender and sexuality, and views on life in general. Changes in all of these areas do have their points of origin in the brain.[15]

Most schools have caved in and reluctantly support the students' uses of devices. In fact, as evidence of succumbing to the tech-immersed generation, teachers are making learning mostly device-driven, with very little deep reading, revised annotating, and handwriting,[16] and in many schools, teachers are deviating from a focus on standardized assessments.[17] Changing brains that are addicted to these changes and, with fixes enabled by schools and leisure, pose a new frontier of challenges on student's brains and emotions, and thus affect student academic development.[18]

THE BRAIN AND STUDENT DEVELOPMENT

Given the scientific understanding of brain development of children and adolescents, several implications for teachers should be considered. First, teachers should understand there are various stages of brain development in students and be able to teach accordingly. They can begin by attending conferences or bringing in experts to present to their districts. This will help provide greater understanding.

Essentially, "the goal of bringing the neuroscience of learning to in-service teachers provides a new perspective on instruction, one where teachers come to see themselves as designers of experiences that ultimately change students' brains . . . [which] is fundamental for anyone assuming a guiding, mentoring, instructive role."[19]

Second, any curriculum that appears as personal should be examined very closely. The same children that would be excited to save an animal, or feed the homeless, would also be just as excited toward other topics, including sexual exploration and experimentation. Opening doors to developing brains brings more curiosity and, with this curiosity, an immediate online search to gratify interest.

There is the risk of experimentation with information that is shared through sexual curriculum at school, with online access to sexual behaviors, and on whether a constant stream of sexual messages breaks down a child's will. The latter is cause for major concern, because grooming by sexual predators occurs similarly. The ease at which students emote today comes with few filters as safeguards.

Curriculum Is More than Words

A study performed in the Netherlands, and published in the *Neuropsychiatric Disease and Treatment* journal, illustrates reasons curriculum that excites the developing brain should be examined very carefully, particularly in adolescents.

> Adolescence is the developmental epoch during which children become adults—intellectually, physically, hormonally, and socially. Adolescence is a tumultuous time, full of changes and transformations. The pubertal transition to adulthood involves both gonadal and behavioral maturation. Magnetic resonance imaging studies have discovered that myelinogenesis, required for proper insulation and efficient neurocybernetics, continues from childhood and the brain's region-specific neurocircuitry remains structurally and functionally vulnerable to impulsive sex, food, and sleep habits. The maturation of the adolescent brain is also influenced by heredity, environment, and sex hormones (estrogen, progesterone, and testosterone), which play a crucial role in myelination. . . . The adolescent population is highly vulnerable to driving under the influence of alcohol and social maladjustments due to an immature limbic system and prefrontal cortex. . . . Adolescents may become involved with offensive crimes, irresponsible behavior, unprotected sex, juvenile courts, or even prison. According to a report by the Centers for Disease Control and Prevention, the major cause of death among the teenage population is due to injury and violence related to sex and substance abuse.[20]

Again, today's students' brains are wiring up differently. The theory that more information about a topic, the better, is now almost obsolete. Cognitive information is now taking a back seat to more activist and emotive curriculum that contains elements of proactivity.

At school and at home, the time spent in front of screens is astounding, and scientists are discovering some very disturbing trends in the brains of Gen Z children.[21] This is not just an American phenomenon. In line with the research out of the Netherlands, some of these changes may be responsible for some of hyper risk-taking we see coming from preteens and teens, in allowing themselves to be involved intimately and taking such risks with teachers.[22] As evidence of this,

> Neuroimaging studies have revealed that when interacting with others and making decisions, adolescents are more likely than adults to be swayed by their emotions. In addition, adolescents often read others' emotions incorrectly. These studies involved comparing a teen brain to an adult brain determined that adolescents' prefrontal cortices are used less often during interpersonal interactions and decision-making than their adult counterparts. In fact, adolescents relied more on the emotional region of their brains when reading others' emotions, which is more impulsive when compared to a logical or measured interpretation.[23]

In addition, "adolescence is one of the most dynamic events of human growth and development, second only to infancy in terms of the rate of development changes that can occur within the brain. . . . In fact, there are characteristic developmental changes that almost all adolescents experience during their transition from childhood to adulthood. It is well established that the brain undergoes a 'rewiring' process that is not complete until approximately 25 years of age."[24] This phenomenon seems to extend the teenage years into the midtwenties, which is why making life-altering decisions in the midst of this chemical turmoil may result from a misreading of any one of several stages of development.

Adolescent immature behaviors are often questioned. The executive functions centered in the prefrontal cortex of the brain are one of the last regions in the brain to develop. This explains why "some adolescents exhibit behavioral immaturity."[25] There are "several executive functions of the human prefrontal cortex that remain under construction during adolescence . . . the fact that brain development is not complete until near the age of 25 years refers specifically to the development of the prefrontal cortex."[26]

In terms of choices made by young people, researchers have developed concepts to apply to the types of thinking that comprise adolescent choices and decisions.

> Researchers have differentiated between "hot" cognition and "cold" cognition. Hot cognition is described as thinking under conditions of high arousal and intense emotion. Under these conditions, teens tend to make poorer decisions. . . . In cold cognition, circumstances are less intense and teens tend to make better decisions. Then, with the addition of complex feelings—such as fear of rejection, wanting to look cool, the excitement of risk, or anxiety, or being caught—it is more difficult for teens to think through potential outcomes, understand the consequences of their decisions, or even use common sense. The apparent immaturity of the connections between the limbic system, prefrontal cortex, and the amygdala provides further support for this concept.[27]

SEXUALITY AND BRAIN DEVELOPMENT

Gen Z is growing up at a very sexually confusing time. Unlike the past, the ability to access information immediately can often lead to greater confusions about a topic. To be told that one can choose a gender that is not the one from birth is in contrast to the cultures of thousands of years of history, hundreds of previous generations, and counter to what the majority of families believe in all nations of the world. This newly advanced theory runs in contrast to all of history, and the norms understood by the medical community stand in stark contrast to the notion.

The rise of digital technology and the internet around the globe also aligns with states of confusion found in other nations. Suddenly, it appears to some that the world is *woke*, when in fact it has just been subjected to an activist's optimizing of a website. The larger question left for further research approaches social movements across the globe. Therefore, the essential macroquestion is *why are these events occurring now with such suddenness?*

One a microlevel, the reason this is such an important discussion is that teachers of different generations will be sharing the same buildings and will have to deal with the strong generational disagreements that may arise over sexuality. Teacher perspectives, curriculum in more progressive states, and personal experiences where one's own children might now question their gender will affect not only what is taught but also how it is taught. The fact that it could be taught to children whose brains and emotions are wrestling daily with development should cause more than a little concern.

Children first discover who they are from their parents, and this identity is reinforced by culture, families and faith, friends, and even physicians. In fact, even with the changes of personal beliefs about gender fluidity, a physician is more likely to treat people by their birth physiology when treatment is required for a medical condition. Imagine how this might add some level of confusion into the mix.

Gender and sexual identity are probably going to go the ways of other issues in American culture. Like *Roe v. Wade* and same-sex marriage, although legal, they will have to be continually forced upon society progressively and politically. This may be the case even as certain issues may never be accepted as morally right or scientifically tenable by a large swath of the American populace. However, in Gen Z there are possibilities of wider-sweeping societal and cultural changes on many fronts.

CHANGES AMONG STUDENTS

Absentee problems, combined with lower assessment and academic proficiency levels, are nothing new. Absenteeism has been a chronic problem year in and year out. Red flags should pop up when students find themselves in college remediation classes, or when they cannot fill out work applications properly, or even make eye contact in interviews. Should the nation be surprised that it is tolerating a culture of illiteracy? Are Americans aware that without enough teachers to step forward to help to turn it around, the situation will continue to worsen?

Changes in Student Accountability

Teachers today cannot grade students as they should be graded. Grade inflation seems to have crept into classrooms. Teachers cannot refer students to the principal's office as they once did, and neither can they discipline students as in years' past, or they can be accused of targeting. Teachers are under the aegis of *safe schools programs* and the exhortation to *graduate students at all cost*.

Education today has become a hotbed of restorative justice and interventions, focusing attention mostly on students of color. This hotbed is the result of data implying certain students are sent out for discipline more often than others. This has led to the axiom that drives the engine of current restorative justice programs: *schools have become pipelines to prison.* Have school officials stopped to consider they are competing against themselves? Students are exhibiting brain development differences from technology use—the likes of which are being fed at the very schools in which students are manifesting troublesome behaviors—and then restricting disciplinary measures in favor of restorative measures. Maybe schools should revisit their policies regarding the uses of devices.

If schools are the conduits by which students wind up in prison, then something is terribly wrong. Meanwhile, with all good intentions, there is great risk in the possibility of the production of false guilt and blame placed upon teachers and other students in classes, because of a notion of latent bias. This can have adverse effects upon students and diminish classroom integrity and student achievements as a result.

Students of any race or background should never feel punished for something for which they are neither aware nor responsible. This type of blame can easily lead to trauma in the lives of all children, if they somehow feel falsely accused or told there are inner prejudices of which they are not aware. Teachers' careers can also be ruined as word spreads that certain schools and teachers are presumed to be racist. Good luck at this point when teacher recruitment is required.

Remedy or Restriction?

An example of seeking remedy for apparent social wrongs is found in the Dolores Huerta Foundation's actions in the state of California. School districts are being monitored to see which students are being disciplined more often by teachers. There is an assumption that students of color are being targeted for discipline more often than other students. This is the assumption even in schools where the minority population is the majority, which raises eyebrows.

Teachers are sensing that they are being accused and targeted themselves, because of the perceived practice of racial targeting of students of color. This pressure has produced toxicity in classrooms that burdens teachers' decision-making every day and diminishes some of their instructional time for all students. No one wins when teachers cannot protect all students and do the jobs to which they were hired.

As a result of this mix of legal and educational concerns, programs focused on behavioral interventions such as Positive Behavioral Interventions and Supports (PBIS) are taking up so much time in classrooms that actual teaching has taken a huge hit. In other words, strategically dealing with problems in-house reduces the referrals, suspensions, and expulsions, to accommodate new behavioral intervention laws. But time will tell if all the work put into keeping Gen Z's troubled students in schools will result in advancing academics and self-regulation of behaviors going forward.

Teachers Beware

Teachers today have to be aware that training in some of these new programs comes with the assumption that they have latent racial biases of which they are unaware. Some teachers are told they might be unknowingly racist in some of their beliefs. Discussions about race have their place, and teachers with adroit and clever skills can walk through these discussions and leave everyone's fragile and even uninformed spirits intact.[28]

How many teachers are walking away from the classrooms because of the school culture that fosters assumptions of latent racism? Teachers just want to teach. Many educators are amazed to discover that back in 2013, teachers of color left the classrooms in greater numbers than their white colleagues.[29] Bureaucrats are aware of this shortage but merely state what is politically expedient.

Public schools need more teachers across the board. In reality, there are serious concerns about the lack of teachers of color to be role models in schools, especially in schools with a large demographic that aligns with the teachers' races or ethnicities. Also of concern are the newer teachers that enter classrooms underscoring the perception that racism is already present in them and that social justice remedies must be applied as part of the classroom management policy and practice.

Amanda Machado illustrates the benefit of a teacher sharing the same racial and ethnic majority of a classroom. She writes,

> The racial identity I shared with my students made me even more sensitive to their struggles, particularly when few other teachers at my school had this same connection. Though 40 percent of students in the American public education system are black and Latino, only 13 percent of teachers nationwide are. In Teach for America specifically, 90 percent of the student corps member

teachers are black and Latino, while 39 percent of corps members are teachers of color. While this lack of proportional diversity exists in several professions, when your job focuses on leading a mostly black and Latino student population to succeed academically and socially in a predominantly white society, race matters so much more.[30]

Studies have shown that students learn best with a teacher who is like them and advocates for them. Machado again illustrates: "To me, racial and social justice was at the core of my work as a teacher. My students' academic progress represented the fate of my racial group, a group I knew had historically been left behind. So at every school meeting, I could only think about how our curriculum and policies ultimately connected to the struggles our students—and I—had faced as people of color."[31] Upon hearing that they are fundamentally disconnected to their students based on race, teachers may begin to doubt their abilities to perform at their highest levels.

Conversely, as students move through the public school system they are smart enough to know there is not much teachers can do to them, in terms of dealing with their behaviors. They understand that most of the laws and policies have them at the center of schooling. At the time of this writing, there are changes being made to discipline guidance policies by the US Department of Education, making attempts to scale back the restrictions on student discipline.

In terms of secondary effects of education policy, the reality is the lack of teacher autonomy in classroom management and discipline have led some teacher-parents to prompt their own children to steer clear of teaching, because of their negative experiences.[32]

THE GRADUATION CULTURE

Recently, a lot of attention was garnered by the number of high school graduates who received their diplomas in 2016. As many are aware, it often takes Herculean efforts to stay involved in the lives of teenagers in order to get them through high school. States and schools are rightfully celebrating their achievements, given that the percentage of graduates had reached an all-time high of around 84 percent in 2016. The 84 percent is based on mathematics adjustments, according to the National Center for Education Statistics.[33]

Incoming freshmen in the class of 2012–2013 comprised the class of 2016. During the 2016 graduation year, the states of Missouri[34] and California[35] had more than a hundred schools each that graduated 100 percent of their 2016 high school senior students. Texas[36] had more than three hundred schools with a 100 percent graduation rate of its 2016 seniors. Conversely, eleven states had no schools with 100 percent graduation in 2016.[37]

The interesting thing, although anecdotal, is that students expelled from high schools had opportunities to graduate from a variety of other schools, including continuation schools, online schools, jail schools while incarcerated, and home study and independent study programs. All of these students, if they graduate from one of the alternative programs, can often be counted as graduates with their original academic class. The program quality and academic rigor of all of these programs are difficult to measure.

What about Dropouts and Absentees?

Dropouts that transferred in after their freshmen year are not usually counted in the graduation number.[38] For example, in California alone,[39] one in ten students dropped out. The numbers of African American dropouts were one in six students.[40] So, where is the actual success? Statistics can be quite deceptive, due to certain exemptions and inclusions not fully described by the numbers.

For example, under the current educational program, the Every Student Succeeds Act (ESSA), students are being graduated even when they violate the attendance policy for graduation eligibility. This culture of student absence is horrific. But what else can a state do when it is under certain guidance rules to graduate students?

According to the US Department of Education, "The timing is ripe for a nationwide reckoning on school attendance,"[41] and here are a few good reasons. In Washington, D.C., about one-third of the entire district's class of 2017 graduated despite policy violations that included excessive absences.[42] In Los Angeles, eighty thousand students missed fifteen or more days of school in 2016.[43] Also in Detroit, more than half of the districts' students have been chronically absent in recent years.[44] Holes are good for Swiss cheese but not good for students' education.

The bottom line on absenteeism is that more than seven million students missed fifteen or more days of school in 2015–2016. That equates to about "16% of the student population, or 1-out-of-six students."[45] Academic progress is slowing down and absentees are missing school, yet percentages of graduates continue to rise. Also on the rise is illiteracy.

THE CULTURE OF ILLITERACY

Anyone in the workplace can see that a high school diploma is worth very little in today's economy. In fact the earning power of the high school diploma is less than a few years ago. Its value is quickly approaching the earning power of a high school dropout,[46] which means it has about the same economic value.

Any culture that reduces the efforts and responsibilities necessary to earn a diploma reduces the overall value of it. Consider that math scores are down again in comparison to those of other nations.[47] The fact is all that is truly needed to graduate high school is to do well in third-grade reading,[48] and these days to attend school irregularly.

Graduation requirements have been drastically reduced, and depending on the state, the average high school student reads at a level somewhere between fifth and sixth grade.[49] Studies found that reading levels generally do not improve dramatically as students move into college.[50] In fact, high school graduates that go on into their freshmen year of college read at a seventh-grade level.[51]

Likewise, staying out of trouble appears to be no longer a prerequisite for at-risk teenagers in order to graduate.[52] Restorative justice programs do their best to see to that. So, what does the employment future hold for those caught in the current graduation culture?

CHANGES IN CAREER AND ECONOMIC CHOICES

Surveys taken of today's college students are revealing that many are choosing to enter majors other than those related to teacher education. Should this excite educators, by keeping the majority of high school graduates away from considering teaching as a career? In so doing two things occur: (1) the supply of teacher education candidates continues to dwindle, and (2) a renewal of the recitation of the old pejorative "Those that can, do. Those that can't, teach."

Career Selection

In 2016, female college students preferred the following majors: (1) business administration and management, (2) biology, (3) criminal justices and corrections, (4) accounting, and (5) general psychology. In terms of the top major from which females graduate, the answer is nursing. More than 120,000 women graduated with a bachelor's degree in nursing in 2016, and the average salary for nurses was about $62,000 annually.[53]

Contrast these numbers with women choosing teacher education as a major and graduate into the teaching ranks. The median salary for female teachers, compared to their classmates who became nurses, ranked a lowly nineteenth out of twenty. The median salary for all teachers in 2016 was about $47,000 annually.[54]

Men of the 2016 graduating class preferred the following top-five majors: (1) business administration and management, (2) general biology, (3) criminal justice and corrections, (4) finance and financial management, and (5) accounting. Mathematics, engineering, and computer science were the fewest preferred, yet yielded the higher salaries. Engineers' salaries ranged from an average of $75,000–$85,000 annually, while computer scientists' annual salaries averaged approximately $75,000.[55]

Teacher education did not appear in the top-twenty list for preferred majors for males and also did not appear on the median salary comparison listing. The median salary for the top-twenty majors chosen by men was $62,060.[56] Aside from any discussion regarding bias, the causes of disparities in salaries, and the selections of college majors, the data are clear. Teacher education, whether elementary or secondary, is an undesirable major for more college students today than in the recent past.

This result is interesting on the one hand, because females still dominate the field of nursing, and males still dominate the fields of engineering and science, but fewer today choose teaching as much as previous generations. A cultural shift has occurred, and more women are pursuing science, technology, engineering, art, and mathematics (STEAM) fields as well as business management. As numbers of students enrolled in schools of education plummet nationally, states will continue to struggle to replace the numbers of teachers needed to fill vacancies.

Shift Away from Teaching

Today's college students are not likely to call teaching their first career option and thus are "less likely to be learning about teaching—and that could be putting future generations' educational attainment at risk."[57] In the year 1975, "more than one-fifth (22 percent) of college students majored in education—a higher share than any other major."[58]

By the year 2015, "fewer than one in 10 Americans pursuing higher education devoted their studies to education. . . . The shift away from an education major was especially notable among women. Over the past 40 years, the share of female college students majoring in education has shrunk from 32 percent to 11 percent. And as interest in a degree in education dwindled, more students pursued coursework in science, fine arts, communications and computer science."[59]

Given that the college population of students is about 58 percent female and 42 percent male, shouldn't there be more women going into teaching?[60] Without the increase of the percentages of women choosing to become teachers, and with women heading into other careers, where do colleges get the candidates to enroll in teacher education programs in colleges?

Incentives to enter education may be so poor for women that they are choosing to earn degrees in other areas that actually pay them less.[61] Rather than go into teaching,[62] it appears younger women today are more willing to sacrifice a bit of money in order to work in a job that allows them to feel fulfilled. Everyone is aware that teachers are not paid handsomely. If money is not an incentive and the demand for teachers is greater than the supply, what is the solution as to how schools of education might attract and retain more students? Subsequent chapters of this book address this very question.

Certainly the demand for teachers is great. Likewise, the number of public school students is trending upward so that public school students are anticipated to swell to more than fifty-five million in less than a decade.[63] Another 10–12 percent of that figure are expected to enroll in private schools. In some states the problem is presently more acute than in other states.[64] Given that a significant population has chosen another profession as a career, and the frightening number of illiterate high school graduates, is there any wonder there are teacher shortages?[65]

A NEW EDUCATION CULTURE

There is truth in the statement that when culture changes, these changes show up very quickly at schools. The culture of the United States has changed drastically since 2000, and more than a few social scientists consider our traditional American culture to be heavily fractured. Depending on political and cultural viewpoints, one can place the blame or the credit for these changes on politicians, presidential administrations, and also the court system.

Society can blame media for the moral decline, or we can blame drugs and substance abuse, and even the continued breakup of the traditional family. Certainly there are multiple factors—not the least of which has affected millions in the nation's education system. All of these factors show up at school every day. As a result, the culture of education has changed significantly.

The Program Panoply

The parade of challenges facing public education today is different than those under No Child Left Behind (NCLB), and even Race to the Top (RTTT). The advent of the Common Core State Standards movement and now the Every Student Succeeds Act (ESSA) has spawned a mini-revolution of sorts in American education. Although in the recent past the federal government had more tightly constrained public education, this is not the current reality.

The reality is that bureaucrats are beginning to loosen some of the stranglehold on education, and in the minds of some, "the nation is finally looking to educators for solutions."[66] In accord with this, the National Education Association (NEA) has introduced seven modern programmatic and practical challenges for public education. These challenges, along with others, are included below:

- Funding for new material, school improvements, technology, curricula, and teachers' salaries and benefits. Some teachers have to work two jobs just to make ends meet for themselves and their families, and others may take more extreme measures.[67]
- School safety. School shootings, drugs, bullying, and violence are major issues.[68]
- Enormous pressure placed on teachers and the new educational environment in which they are expected to thrive. Along with the workload of teaching, grading, and student facilitation, the roles of teachers have increased. They are now focusing more on student problems within counselor roles, dealing with more classroom management social and emotional issues of students, and under pressure to reduce referrals and suspensions, while at the same time increase graduation rates.[69]
- The pressure of social media. Students take to social media to post about teachers and use their phones to contact parents, which then brings near-immediate responses and immediate pressures on teachers. There is a real concern that student cell phone addiction is problematic inside the classroom.[70]
- Teacher illnesses and injuries. Anxiety, emotional disorders, depression, burnout, and injury are among the serious mental health concerns that add to teacher attrition.
- Teachers are unable to consider the discipline of students as they have done in the past. The policies have changed, and programs have been instituted to keep more and more students on campuses, instead of suspending them, or even expelling them for poor or violent behaviors. Some teachers report that they feel undermined and their authority has been thwarted by these discipline policy shifts by some states.
- Student absenteeism is a real concern. Students that miss even one day of school a week miss 20 percent of their education.
- Standardized assessments that hold teachers accountable, when there are serious gaps in the learning of their students, place added pressures on teachers—especially in states where a teacher's evaluation can include student assessment scores.
- Undocumented students who are in the country illegally have been a flashpoint for those outside of education. The Deferred Action for Childhood Arrivals (DACA) has become an issue that has marginalized Americans. Funding is allocated for public schools, and it has become a right for all students in American public schools to receive an education. That being said, public school teachers are under enormous pressure to educate children from other nations and language groups, regardless of their citizenship status.
- Teacher attrition is rising, and teacher education candidates are not readily jumping into the replacement pipeline for those who are leaving for rea-

sons other than retirement. The rise of temporary licensed and emergency credentialed teachers, along with those holding other permitted alternative certifications, is cause for concern. Untrained teachers are showing up in more and more schools in the United States. This does very little to answer the critics of education, as well as advocates of educational equity.
- Along with new smartphone applications, new educational and game technologies are claiming the attention of America's students, as well as frustrating teachers. There are always promises of the best educational technology, or that assessment scores improve a certain percentage by using a new technology in class. Technology is a tool, and teachers should determine how this technology should be best used in the classroom. Employers clamor for the skills that are not being taught so readily any longer in schools.[71]
- Advocates for school choice, charters, and private schools are challenging the value of traditional public education. The implications are that millions of students are being siphoned off to attend schools other than the traditional public institutions. When that happens, the funds often follow. The NEA has asked public school teachers and their associations to fight what they see as a movement to undermine the mission of public education.[72]
- Rapidly rising numbers of special education students and special needs students included in traditional classrooms have added additional pressures on teachers who are untrained in working with these students, or lack proper credentials to work in such an environment.
- Public education has become more polarized. Teachers are being encouraged to run for political office, and others are being rallied to vote out lawmakers who do not favor public education as it is favored by the NEA and other national and local education groups.[73]

A SHIFT IN HIGHER EDUCATION

The reality is government institutions both making the laws and interpreting the laws are the places where our nation finds the genesis of large cultural shifts. Education policy cannot escape these shifts. Schooling succumbs to the decisions of court cases, threats by groups with political agendas, and certainly from actions of political parties.

Education, it seems, is always in the crosshairs. Whether by bureaucrats or by extremely radical groups,[74] the effects of actions taken are not lost on our nation's children. What happens at the higher levels of college bureaucracy ultimately finds its way into public schools.

An example of this is the recent discussion in higher education about grading methods. There are some that think the current method of grading is an example of racial supremacy and that grading students through this lens is a standard based on racism and white nationalism. Consider the following remarks that were given at a recent conference.

The Write Stuff?

At the 2019 American University conference, titled "Grading Ain't Just Grading: Rethinking Writing Assessment Ecologies towards Antiracist Ends,"[75] Professor Asao B. Inoue presented the argument for the grading of student writing as oppressive and evidence of "white supremacy."[76]

Inoue's plenary session, "The Language Standards that Kill Our Students: Grading Ain't Just Grading," argued "against the use of conventional standards in college courses that grade student writing by single standards."[77] Inoue discussed "the ways that White language supremacy is perpetuated in college classrooms despite the better intentions of faculty, particularly through the practices of grading writing."[78] Breakout sessions included other provocative topics, such as "Creating Antiracist Writing Assessment Ecologies in Writing Courses, and Problem-Posing the Nature of Judgement in Writing Intensive Courses."[79]

The lowering of writing standards cannot lead to better writing, as viewed especially in the errors found on the conference website. Ask any elementary or middle school teacher whose job it is to make certain that "ask is not ax," and the word "like" is not used adjectivally. However, in today's hyper-emotional climate, certainly relying on the argument that anything smacks of racial supremacy is sure to find an audience.

Are Standards Racist?

The position that having a standard from which to grade is oppressive to lesser-educated students may in itself be racist by default. Labeling children as oppressed and lowering standards to meet one's definition of oppression is the kind of soft bigotry that rears its ugly head from time to time.

Teachers are well aware of the phrase coined by Michael Gerson "the soft bigotry of low expectations."[80] Advancing the perspective that grading students according to a standard is somehow connected to racism is to miss a major point.

If there is a racial supremacy to writing, then why not one for western Common Core mathematics, reading and literature, next-gen science, art, music, etc.? If racism is in everything, then such an argument defeats the point at its origin. Is everything in education to be construed as toxic to one group or another?[81] Can our nation just support teachers and allow them just to teach?

Scaling back the correcting of students' writing means reducing one's professorial expertise to lower levels of knowledge and understanding. Computers might as well destroy their own spell-check utilities. Hovering at those levels would lack appeal to any rigorous taxonomy in education. But publishers do not seek this. Writers of technical documents do not want this. Employers that read job applications do not desire lower standards.

The real worlds of business and law do not want lower standards either. Consider what if mathematics, physics, and engineering professors are willing to reduce absolute answers in order to reward students' best efforts? Should they be concerned about sociologists' theories on white supremacy as they evaluate the sufficiency of their students and calculation proficiency? The building of bridges by anyone whose math was not corrected is quite scary, let alone those built by supposed engineers.

Blinded by Whiteness?

Baby boomer's perspectives on racism and bigotry were formed while Jim Crow was still practiced in several states. Personal recollections of a time where policies and laws were punitive and restrictive based on the color of one's skin, and the subsequent practices of separation and inequality, are painful reminders of a horrible period of American history.

Going after these problems was the right thing to do. In some corners of this nation, there is still a lot that could be done to continue the progress toward racial equality. Changing mindsets that are stuck in hate or prejudice may not ever be achieved, and that is sad. Yet, Gen Z has a fighting chance.

In some areas of the nation, people are still living as they did in the 1960s. In other areas of the nation racial progress is very noticeable. Whether socially, economically, professionally, and educationally, advantages have been realized for racial minorities all over this nation. Yet, there are those that experience racism just as realistically as it was experienced in the 1950s and 1960s. Contemporary experiences may well trigger deep-seated intergenerational traumas. To what extent are schools meant to be the crucibles for repairing society's ills? Is the best way to continue to progress to use teachers as activists?

Although policies and laws helped to diminish the actions of racism in society, there is a major difference today with those claiming racism, particularly coming from colleges and universities. In the past, racism was practiced more openly. Today, the claim is that racism is latent and most Caucasian people today are *blinded by whiteness and privilege.*

Where racism is not openly displayed, the motivation of some people can now be challenged. The theory maintains that most white people are not even aware of the racism that resides in their psyches. In fact, when approached with this very notion that people can harbor racism unknowingly, it is difficult for people to fathom. Teaching such theories to children may damage their own self-esteem and cause them to doubt their own identities.

Is this the new type of thinking that Americans want to become pervasive in public schools? If so, then every time a student disagrees with someone, or questions another student, it may well lead to the conclusion that a person's latent belief in racial superiority is the cause. This is not good for the future of American students and certainly will not attract more teachers into classrooms.

Critics see this as accusatory by placing claims of racism on many who are Caucasian. Critics also claim that empowering teachers to instruct children about latent racism is to leave children worse off, in terms of their own esteem and existence. Others see it differently. Laurie Calvert, a progressive Democrat and former Obama campaign supporter, sees value in coming to terms with her latent racism. She writes about the moments she was made aware of latent racism in her own life, in her article titled "I Was a Racist Teacher and I Didn't Even Know It."[82]

HOW DESPERATE ARE AMERICAN SCHOOLS?

Some argue that the American public education system in the United States has become too bloated and overburdened. Along with salient other issues addressed in this chapter, it is said that the public school system is far too large to succeed. Cash-cradling school districts and bloated administrative entities, with political allies that promise to serve people *from cradle-to-career*,[83] cannot sustain themselves any longer. Still, politicians think that spending more money on problems fixes these problems. One only has to look to the culture that is created by this thinking.

Political expediency aside, the American education system has not been sustainable for a while. The system is hemorrhaging from self-imposed wounds. Students and their families are choosing different educational pathways to avoid any contagion. Teachers are leaving their careers in record numbers.

The problem is so severe in some places that states are finding ways to support the growing number of people looking elsewhere to educate their children. States are officially recognizing alternatives to public education.[84] But politicians have to be on guard to avoid appearing to be all in, for the sake of political expediency.[85]

The elephant in the room is that for the first time, "a majority of Americans now support the expansion of school choice for all families."[86] This fact does little to invigorate a resurgence of energy in the direction of public education. The truth is education culture is broken and schools are collateral damage.

The Inner Cities

Frank Igwe of the *Harvard Crimson* illustrates the state of America's broken education system:

> This is . . . what is happening in America's inner-city school system, and is a reality for many of the children who attend such schools. The teachers, and many students, realize that the educational system is failing them, and that they are ill prepared to face the real world beyond graduation. As one principal remarked, "Where the schools fail, the streets will take over," and all involved parties can only look on with a sense of helplessness, caught in a diabolical waiting game as the schools and the streets vie for the hearts and mind of the children.[87]

Where some bureaucrats see progress, others see corruption. Jack Schneider asks, "[Do] policy leaders and stakeholders accelerate the pace of development? Probably. Can the schools do more to realize national ideals around equity and inclusion? Without question. But none of these aims will be achieved by ripping the system apart. That's a ruinous fiction. The struggle to create great schools for all young people demands swift justice and steady effort, not melodrama and magical thinking."[88] Is there hope for the future? Without adequate staffing of qualified teachers, there is little hope of repair.

The following list includes areas where there is consensus among researchers that American culture is broken and affecting American public school students.[89] The areas of concern include the following:

- Nuclear family structure
- Politics, mainstream and radical
- Civil discourse
- The ability to converse about competing values
- Problem-students school inclusion
- Mental illness and drug addiction
- Personal and group identity movements and pressures upon teachers to advocate
- Individualism versus common good
- Growing number of untrained teachers
- Increases in violence in schools against teachers and students
- Academically advanced students sheltered in exclusive programs
- Public school students fleeing to charter schools, private schools, or homeschools
- Disagreements that result in hateful labels
- Polarized nation over issues of family, morality, facts, truth, and lifestyles
- Bias in media feeding raw emotions and polarization

- Schools and teachers becoming advocates and activists against groups and their issues
- Programs focus less on discipline and more on emotions
- Rampant accusations of racism
- Demonization of wealth
- College admission practicing equity of competition and not by purchase by privilege
- Social and emotional learning programs reducing academic time
- Athletics over academics
- Grade inflation and grade adjustments to keep students eligible for activities and sports
- Illiteracy and high school graduation rates
- Education equity and reducing merit-based recognition

Many of the items on the list above are put into perspective by Kay Hymowitz, as she writes about one fundamental reality found in all cultures: "If America wants to begin somewhere, and move toward some real repair of those places where people meet each day by the millions and millions, then support the nuclear family. The nuclear family wasn't born after the Industrial Revolution."[90]

Teachers today are looking at rearing other people's children in schools well beyond the scope of their calling and employment. They are becoming more and more like surrogate parents and agents of social change. Students from broken families attending broken schools that revolve around a broken system have little hope of touching their potential, and in the words of Ed Boland, "broken schools can't be saved by hero teachers."[91] However, there is a cautious optimism afoot: Millennials are just now waking up to this reality.

INCENTIVIZING HOPE FOR THE FUTURE

Millennials are going to have to be provided serious incentives to attract them from raising their own young families to stepping into today's public school classrooms to be surrogates for others' families. They may choose to do so en masse, because "the nuclear family is more adaptable and more child-centered than the traditional extended family clan."[92] However, they may choose to center on their own children instead. The fact is, "in all, more than 17 million Millennial women have become mothers."[93] But what will attract some of these millions into public school classrooms?

In 2016, "Millennial women accounted for 82% of U.S. births."[94] Will there be enough of an economic incentive for them to leave their children in the care of others each day, or drop them off at a local public school that is mediocre at best? The chances are great that as the idealists in both the Millennial and Z generations rear their children, they are going to choose what is best for them. Will public education be part of their options?

That being said, not all teachers that remain in today's public school classrooms went into those classrooms to raise other parents' children. Elizabeth Mulvahill of We Are Teachers contends, "Teachers are a particularly tenacious lot, but some teachers are leaving because they have decided to invest their energy closer to home. . . . Heather A. expressed her disappointment this way: 'I realized that the school system is broken beyond repair. Years and years of spackle and duct tape just can't hold it together anymore. When you realize that you wouldn't send your own children to your school . . . you quit and homeschool them.'"[95]

CONCLUSION

Schools cannot fix what is broken in the families in the United States. Schools cannot fix what is broken socially in the United States. Families in America want the best for their children. People from all over the world come to the United States, and some take desperate measures—even illegal ones—to bring their families here for better lives. There is something very appealing about our system. Most often this appeal is economic. How sad it would be if this incentive was not enough to increase the supply of teachers, especially in states with disproportionate and disparate salaries.

Americans live now in an era when political foes tear into each other just to win elections. They rip each other apart for having too many resources and argue about inequity. The nation also lives at a time when the 24-7 news cycle has become a basis for political advocacy on all sides. Brazen teachers also tend to speak to the margins in culture. For the most part, teachers signed up to teach and to watch students gain the skills they will need as they head into adulthood.

America now has a more activist-oriented culture, and teacher advocates for one position or another are found in classrooms all over the United States. As political and social activism continue to rise in schools, academics continue to drop. American culture comes to school embedded in each of the psyches of children. Teachers sense all of these pressures and view many of the visual effects on students. Some teachers even take on these pressures personally.

Whatever is part of culture can be expected to show its face in schools, and that means that someone or something is always in the bureaucratic crosshairs. In this new culture of teacher shortages, it is teachers who are far too often the targets of educational woes. So, how do states attract and support new teachers in genuine ways?

NOTES

1. C. S. Lewis, *The Abolition of Man* (New York: HarperCollins, 2001), 13.
2. Octavio Javier Esqueda, "What Every Church Needs to Know about Generation Z," *Talbot Magazine*, 2018, 12.
3. Lewis, *Abolition of Man*, chaps. 1, 3. Cf. "The Poison of Subjectivism," Lessons from C. S. Lewis, 2005, https://probe.org.
4. Esqueda, "What Every Church Needs," 13.
5. Ibid.
6. Ibid.
7. Ibid.
8. Ibid.
9. Ibid., 13–14.
10. Ibid., 14.
11. Ibid.
12. Ibid.
13. Benedict Carey, "Is Screen Time Bad for Kids' Brains?" *New York Times*, December 10, 2018, https://www.nytimes.com.
14. Victoria L. Dunckley, "Screentime Is Making Kids Moody, Crazy and Lazy," *Psychology Today*, August 18, 2015, https://www.psychologytoday.com.
15. "Brain Architecture," Harvard University Center on the Developing Child, 2019, https://developingchild.harvard.edu.
16. John Rosales, "The Racist Beginnings of Standardized Testing," *NEA Today*, Spring 2018, http://www.nea.org.
17. Valerie Strauss, "34 Problems with Standardized Tests," *Washington Post*, April 19, 2017, https://www.washingtonpost.com.
18. Joan Twenge, "Too Much Screen Use Really Might Change Your Kid's Brain," *Live Science*, December 18, 2018, https://www.livescience.com.
19. Janet M. Dubinsky, Gillian Roehrig, and Sashank Varma, "Infusing Neuroscience into Teacher Professional Development," *Educational Researcher* 42, no. 6 (August–September): 317–29, https://www.ncbi.nlm.nih.gov.
20. Mariam Arain, Maliha Haque, Lina Johal, et al., "Maturation of the Adolescent Brain," *Neuropsychiatric Disease and Treatment* 9 (2013): 449–61, https://www.ncbi.nlm.nih.gov.
21. Anderson Cooper, "Groundbreaking Study Examines Effects of Screen Time on Kids," *60 Minutes*, December 9, 2018, https://www.cbsnews.com.
22. Arain, Haque, Johal, et al., "Maturation of the Adolescent Brain."
23. Ibid.
24. Ibid.
25. Ibid.
26. Ibid.
27. Ibid.
28. Jeffrey R. Young, "How Classrooms Can Start Talking about Race in Just 6 Words," EdSurge, November 1, 2018, https://www.edsurge.com.
29. Amanda Machado, "Why Teachers of Color Quit," *Atlantic*, December 23, 2013, https://www.theatlantic.com.
30. Ibid.
31. Ibid.
32. Maureen Downey, "New Poll: Majority of Parents Don't Want Their Kids to Become Teachers," *Atlanta-Journal Constitution*, August 28, 2018, https://www.ajc.com.
33. "Public High School Graduation Rates," National Center for Education Statistics, May 2018, https://nces.ed.gov.
34. Briana Boyington, "See High School Graduation Rates by States," *U.S. News and World Report*, May 18, 2018, https://www.usnews.com.
35. Ibid.
36. Ibid.
37. Ibid.

38. Ibid.
39. John Fensterwald, "California's Graduation Rate Ticks Up but, Still, 1 in 10 High School Students Drops Out," *EdSource*, November 27, 2018, https://edsource.org.
40. Ibid.
41. Taylor Swaak, "Education Plans: Will It Make a Difference?" *The 74*, July 31, 2018, https://www.the74million.org.
42. Katie McGee, "In D.C., 34 Percent of Graduates Received a Diploma against District Policy," *nprED* , January 29, 2018, https://www.npr.org.
43. Anna M. Phillips, "How L.A. Unified Could Reduce Absenteeism, If It Listens to Outside Advisors," *Los Angeles Times*, December 5, 2017, https://www.latimes.com.
44. Jennifer Chambers, "Schools Grapple with More Students Cutting Class," *Detroit News*, December 12, 2017, https://www.detroitnews.com.
45. "Chronic Absenteeism in the Nation's Schools," *US Department of Education*, October 27, 2016, https://www2.ed.gov.
46. Jillian Berman, "A High-School Diploma Is Pretty Much Useless These Days," *Huffington Post*, December 6, 2017, https://www.huffingtonpost.com. Cf. Kevin Mahnken, "More HS Students Are Graduating, but These Key Indicators Prove Those Diplomas Are Worth Less than Ever," *The 74*, March 26, 2017, https://www.the74million.org.
47. Theresa Harrington, "U.S. Math Scores Decline on International Test of 15-Year-Olds," *EdSource*, December 5, 2016, https://edsource.org.
48. Grace Chen, "Third Grade Reading Correlates with High School Graduation Rates," *Public School Review*, December 1, 2017, https://www.publicschoolreview.com. Cf. Sarah D. Sparks, "Study: Third Grade Reading Predicts Later High School Graduation," *Education Week*, April 8, 2011, http://blogs.edweek.org.
49. "American High School Students Are Reading Books at 5th-Grade Appropriate Levels: Report," *Huffington Post*, March 23, 2012, https://www.huffingtonpost.com. Cf. Hector Tobar, "American Adults Have Low (and Declining) Reading Proficiency," *Los Angeles Times*, October 5, 2013, https://www.latimes.com.
50. Natalie Wexler, "Why American Students Haven't Gotten Better at Reading in 20 Years," *Atlantic*, April 13, 2018, https://www.theatlantic.com.
51. Jason Amos, "Nation's Report Card Shows Little Progress in Reading and Math—Except on This Measure," *Alliance for Excellent Education*, April 11, 2018, https://all4ed.org. Cf. Merrill Hope, "Expert: Most US College Freshmen Read at 7th Grade Level," *Breitbart*, January 3, 2015, https://www.breitbart.com.
52. June Kronholz, "Getting At-Risk Teens to Graduation," *Education Next* 11, no. 4 (Fall 2011): 24–31, https://www.educationnext.org. Cf. "Across the Stage: Doing What It Takes to Help Every Student Graduate from High School," *American Federation of Teachers*, 2012, https://www.aft.org.
53. "The Most Popular Majors for Women and Men," *College Factual: The U.S. Department of Education Data*, November 22, 2017, https://inside.collegefactual.com.
54. Ibid.
55. Ibid.
56. Ibid.
57. Jacob Passy, "Why America's Teacher Shortage Is Going to Get Worse," *New York Post*, February 14, 2018, https://nypost.com.
58. Ibid.
59. Ibid.
60. Beth Greenwood, "Teacher Pay versus Nursing Pay," *Chron*, accessed May 7, 2019, https://work.chron.com.
61. "The Most Popular Majors for Women and Men," *College Factual*, November 22, 2017.
62. Ernest J. Zarra III, *The Entitled Generation: Helping Teachers Teach and Reach the Minds and Hearts of Generation Z* (Lanham, MD: Rowman & Littlefield, 2017).
63. "Fast Facts: Enrollment Trends," US Department of Education National Center for Education Statistics, 2018, https://nces.ed.gov. Cf. US Department of Education, National Center for Education Statistics, *Digest of Education Statistics*, 2016, chap. 1.

64. Diane Rado, "Top Ten States Expecting Drops in Public School Enrollment," *Forbes*, April 19, 2018, https://www.forbes.com.
65. Tiffany Munro, "12 Countries with the Highest Percentage of Female High School Teachers," *World Atlas*, April 25, 2017, https://www.worldatlas.com.
66. Amanda Litvinov, Brenda Alvarez, Cindy Long, et al., "10 Challenges Facing Public Education Today," *NEA Today*, August 3, 2018, http://neatoday.org.
67. Madeline Will, "To Make Ends Meet, 1 in 5 Teachers Have Second Jobs," *Education Week*, June 19, 2018, https://www.edweek.org.
68. "Safe Youth, Safe Schools," National Center for Injury Prevention and Control, Division of Violence Prevention and Centers for Disease Control and Prevention, August 4, 2017, https://www.cdc.gov.
69. "Reenvisioning the Teacher as a Maker: 9 Roles for the Teacher that Leads," *TeachThought*, August 20, 2017, https://www.teachthought.com. Cf. Judith Taack Lanier, "Redefining the Role of the Teacher: It's a Multifaceted Profession," *Edutopia: The George Lucas Educational Foundation*, July 1, 1997, https://www.edutopia.org. Cf. also Sam Sandate, "How I'm Tackling the Stress and Suicidal Thoughts of America's Public School Students," *Yahoo Finance*, February 4, 2019, https://finance.yahoo.com.
70. Steve Gardiner, "The Student Cellphone Addiction Is No Joke," *Education Week*, April 26, 2016, https://www.edweek.org.
71. Diane Schaffhauser, "Employers Want 'Uniquely Human Skills,'" *Campus Technology*, January 17, 2019, https://campustechnology.com.
72. "NEA Adopts Charter School Policy Statement," *NEA*, July 4, 2017, https://ra.nea.org.
73. Maya Riser-Kositsky, Madeline Will, and Daarel Burnette II, "Over 170 Teachers Ran for State Office in 2018. Here's What We Know About Them," *Education Week*, November 21, 2018, https://www.edweek.org.
74. "Education in the Crosshairs: Thoughts on the New Student Movement," Solidarity: A Socialist, Feminist, Anti-Racist Organization, September 24, 2010, https://solidarity-us.org.
75. Asao Inoue, "Grading Ain't Just Grading: Rethinking Writing Assessment Ecologies toward Antiracist Ends," American University, February 1, 2019, https://edspace.american.edu. Cf. Tom Ciccotta, "American University Tells Faculty to Disregard 'Quality' of Writing When Grading," *Breitbart*, January 11, 2019, https://www.breitbart.com.
76. Ibid.
77. Ibid.
78. Ibid.
79. Ibid.
80. George W. Bush, "President Bush Addresses NAACP Annual Convention," White House, July 20, 2006, https://georgewbush-whitehouse.archives.gov. Cf. Martin Wren, "The Soft Bigotry of Low Expectation," Employment First, 2019, https://employmentfirst.com/.
81. "Is Your School's Culture Toxic or Positive?" *Education World*, accessed May 7, 2019, https://www.educationworld.com.
82. Laurie Calvert, "I Was a Racist Teacher and I Didn't Even Know It," *Education Post*, August 24, 2017, https://educationpost.org.
83. "From Cradle to Career: Newsom's Vision For Education Reform in California," *EdSource*, June 6, 2018, https://edsource.org.
84. John Haughey, "DeSantis Vows to Eliminate School Choice Voucher Waiting List at MLK Event," *Florida WatchDog*, January 22, 2019, https://www.watchdog.org.
85. Alia Wong, "Public Opinion Shifts in Favor of School Choice," *Atlantic*, August 21, 2018, https://www.theatlantic.com.
86. Ibid.
87. Frank Igwe, "Broken Schools," *Harvard Crimson*, February 1, 2010, https://www.thecrimson.com.
88. Jack Schneider, "America's Not-So Broken Education System: Do U.S. Schools Really Need to Be Disrupted?" *Atlantic*, June 22, 2016, https://www.theatlantic.com.
89. Matthew Lynch, "10 Reasons the U.S. Education System Is Failing," *EdWeek*, August 27, 2015, http://blogs.edweek.org.

90. Kay Hymowitz, "The Real Roots of the Nuclear Family," *Institute for Family Studies*, December 23, 2013, https://ifstudies.org.

91. Ed Boland, "Broken Schools Cannot Be Saved by Hero Teachers," *Newsweek*, May 10, 2016, https://www.newsweek.com.

92. Hymowitz, "Real Roots."

93. Gretchen Livingston, "More than a Million Millennials Are Becoming Moms Each Year," *Pew Research Center*, May 4, 2018, http://www.pewresearch.org.

94. Ibid.

95. Elizabeth Mulvahill, "Why Good Teachers Quit Teaching: Burnout Is Real," *We Are Teachers*, January 4, 2018, https://www.weareteachers.com.

Chapter Two

Vanishing Passion

> Managers in many professions—including those working for school systems—share a common topic of complaint these days: challenges around hiring and keeping millennials.[1]

Statistics indicate that with the current teacher shortage, there are some geographic regions hyper-desperate in their needs for teachers. These are described by the US Department of Education as Teacher Shortage Areas (TSAs). The definition of a shortage area is "a subject matter or grade level within a state in which there is an inadequate supply of elementary or secondary teachers. A shortage may be caused by teaching positions that are unfilled by teachers who have temporary certification or teach in an academic subject other than their area of preparation."[2]

There are serious concerns about the number of teachers just calling it quits or finding other employment to make ends meets. Teachers all over the nation are at their wit's end with students, parents, and even the system of education itself. Essentially, their passion for teaching has dissipated, and in some cases has vanished altogether. Reflecting this phenomenon is Tracy, a twenty-nine-year teaching veteran. She writes, "After 29 years, I don't want to go there! I've nearly had a breakdown. I had to go on meds, and cry daily. I've been teacher of the year 3 times. I'm a good teacher. I can't quit. I have one more year to get my retirement. What is happening? It's everywhere. It breaks my heart."[3]

Tracy is not alone in experiencing the vortex of dissipation of passion. America's young people are drawing closer to the workforce in a variety of ways. Teaching is not among their burning interests.

EYES FINALLY OPEN

Just a few years ago, education researchers proclaimed that there was no shortage of teachers in America. In fact, they claimed that the problem was one of perception surrounding equity, in terms of teacher distribution. Some still echo this claim today.

Heather Voke writes, "Researchers . . . dispute the conventional wisdom that the shortage exists because there are simply not enough qualified teachers to fill the number of vacant positions. If we consider only the number of qualified candidates and the number of job openings, there is an overall surplus."[4] Some educators find it next to impossible to believe that teachers would just begin to lose interest in their jobs and close the doors on their careers.

Certainly in a general sense, every *teacher-trained* person—even those retired—could be considered in the surplus and be counted accordingly. However, now that bureaucrats' eyes are opening more widely, reality cannot be reasoned away. The reality is that currently people are not being trained to enter the field of teaching to match the new openings of K–12 schools, or to replace those who simply walked away.

MAIN REASONS TEACHERS WANT OUT OF TEACHING

No one likes employment crises. Teachers are no different than any other worker with a career when it comes to a crisis. The US teaching ranks are at crisis levels. "The country is facing an education crisis as more teachers leave the profession for other fields, often lured by higher pay. At the same time, colleges have witnessed a plunge in the ranks of students majoring in education, leading to a shrinking pipeline of young classroom teachers."[5]

The Learning Policy Institute explains: "The teacher shortage emerged in the wake of the Great Recession, when school districts cut their staffing as funding dried up. But student enrollment has only grown, adding to the pressures on local schools. At the same time, fewer college students are opting to become teachers because of the economics of college debt."[6]

Linda Darling-Hammond adds, "People can't stay in a profession where they can't afford to support their families."[7] As a result, "the numbers of teachers leaving the profession for other fields has grown. . . . Most leave for jobs in health care or social assistance, which includes nursing, family assistance and child care."[8]

There are less and less students enrolling in education and teacher education programs nationally. "Enrollments dropped by 35 percent between 2009 and 2014, according to the Learning Policy Institute,"[9] and today's teachers are "earning almost 2 percent less that they did in 1999 and 5 percent less that their 2009 pay, according to the Department of Education."[10] It will take much more than Learning Policy Institute recommendations to reverse the trend.

The Critical Need Areas

In terms of the loss rates and turnovers of teachers, the "rates are highest in the South and lowest in the Northeast, where states tend to offer higher pay, support smaller class sizes, and make greater investments in education. Shortages also persist in specific areas: mathematics, science, special education, English language development, and foreign languages and turnover rates are 50% higher in Title I schools, which serve more low-income students."[11]

Turnover rates are also "70% higher for teachers in schools serving the largest concentrations of students of color,"[12] but areas of "most every state in America face troubling teacher shortages: the most frequent shortage areas are math, science, bilingual education and special education."[13]

Teachers who get locked into a community where the cost of living is greater have a more difficult time walking away from their higher-paying teaching jobs, although their higher salaries do not actually give them any real economic advantage. This is also true with teachers with families that are deeply enmeshed in communities. The fact that they stay does not imply they wouldn't leave if the economics worked in their favor. The economic risk may be greater by proportion in the Northeast than it is in the South, yet attrition is affecting all regions.

The issue that current policy analysts are not addressing is the variation in commitment levels resident in the different generations in today's workplace. Millennials and Gen Z workers view the struggles of teachers very differently. Job satisfaction and potential growth are important. One Gen Z teacher remarked, "Why should I teach and raise other people's kids? That doesn't leave much time or energy for my own."

Another very important critical need is placing today's generation of young people as teachers into our schools when they are given to making swift-change career choices. With this in mind, can any such generation be counted as deeply passionate about their jobs?

What so-called profession, when there is great demand for workers, offers disincentives for those who wish to join or remain in the profession? Rather than increasing salaries and benefits, as every other legitimate profession does when the demand for professionals is high and the supply is low, public education simply finds ways to try to increase the supply by manipulating credential requirements, relaxing the strict requirements for certification, and then looking outside of schools of education to fill local public school classrooms. The vortex continues to swirl.

Warm Bodies as Professionals

Dropping requirements is not enhancing the quality of the supply of teachers. Gen Z does not want to board a sinking ship. This is only an incentive to increase numbers and not an incentive to increase quality. In other words, it is a reason to refer to teaching as anything but a profession. In some places in America, it seems that school districts would be better off running a temp agency for short-term workers' contracts.

The need is for warm bodies, and the reality is just having vacancies filled is enough to calm the bureaucracy—but the public should be outraged! This kind of outlook and approach should not be viewed as unintended consequences for states like California and Virginia, where the Democratic governors initially banned education as a major at college. There is no genius in limiting education majors in colleges and then expecting numbers of applicants to rise to fill the void we now face.

The good news is some states committed to this trimming have since reversed their policies and reinstated education as a major.[14] However, is it too little, too late? Governors come and governors go, but the lasting effects of education policy are more than gubernatorial—they are generational. For a list of teacher vacancies and positions filled by teachers holding one or more alternate credentials, see appendix A.

Leaky Bucket Syndrome

Examples of shifting policies to cover for mistakes in judgment for missing the markers of the current shortage of teachers include Virginia, California, Oklahoma, Arizona, Illinois, and Minnesota. States are now resorting to passing emergency regulations to streamline education requirements for the hiring of new teachers. States are using their own strategies "to increase the number of new teachers by lowering the teacher licensure requirements."[15] This is not good news,[16] and it certainly is not good governmental management. Stopgap measures are used during crises—which should reveal a lot about the general condition of American education.

In an effort to step up hiring to remedy what appears as an act of desperation, New York State "allowed charter schools to certify their own teachers and dropped literacy tests for teacher candidates."[17] The bucket that used to be full of teachers just waiting for openings in schools has been leaking for years. The cultural changes in education and American culture are now rearing desperate measures. The nation can no longer afford bureaucrats the opportunity to manage this crisis.

NPR's Eric Westervelt and Kat Lonsdorf describe the "leaky bucket" phenomenon, as they write, "The teaching force is a leaky bucket, losing hundreds of thousands of teachers each year—a majority of them before retirement age. . . . The 'I'm outta here' rate is an estimated 8 percent a year—twice that of high-performing countries like Finland and Singapore. And that . . . is a lot higher than other professions."[18] The persistent dripping has taken its toll.

Dollars and Sense

The knowledge is common that there are many reasons that teachers are driven away from classrooms. To review, some of these include money, the lack of a say in how education should proceed, working conditions, lack of support by administrators, and other time for academic preparation to do their jobs as teachers.

Still, some teachers remain, and there are good schools and districts where the hemorrhaging of teachers is not as acute.[19] However, isolation from massive national cultural changes is short-lived. When culture changes, these changes have profound effects upon schools across the land.

In 2018, there were about 231 "voluntary departures per 10,000 workers" in public education.[20] Cultural changes in education policy bring implications upon the social fabric of society, enter the pipeline of downward momentum, within which most have little choice but to yield to the movement. The culture of the recent past that would have attracted new teachers to exciting careers has been working against itself for at least two decades.

This trend downward in available teachers is so concerning that there are no indications of its slowing any time in the near future. Students at college are not showing great interest in pursuing careers in education. They look at the compensation and reply, "No thanks!" There is also a culture change in the minds of contemporary Millennial and Gen Z women. The voices of culture are being heard loudly and clearly. "The shift away from an education major was especially notable among women. Over the past 40 years, the interest in a degree in education has shrunk from 32 percent to 11 percent. As interest in a degree in education dwindled, more students pursued coursework in science, fine arts, communications and computer science."[21] Passion for education is quickly being replaced with exciting new STEM (science, technology, engineering, and mathematics) possibilities, along with better pay too. Finances speak their own cultural language. These new passions do not bode well for the prospects of young people becoming teachers.

Same Old, Same Old?

The critics would argue that this all has happened before and just getting through this period of shortage would again lead to another boom for teacher education enrollments. An answer to such criticism is that when culture shifts education policy, the effects are wide sweeping. An analysis of the drivers of public school teacher shortages extends to all levels. The fact is that along with teachers, "community-college faculty, school psychologists and janitors, are quitting their jobs at the fastest rate on record."[22] These are not all retiring baby boomers. To reiterate, there are some things that are definitely wrong within the culture of American public education, and so far, education policymakers do not have an answer to a problem they helped to create.

Labor statistics show that of the ten million Americans who work in public education across all categories and titles, one in ten left their jobs in 2018. About "one million workers quit public-education positions" mostly to head into other employment.[23] Although teachers have walked away from jobs in the past for a variety of economic and personal reasons, "quitting among public educators stands out because the field is one where stability is viewed as a key perk and longevity often rewarded."[24] This is no longer the case.

Whether poor pay, the inability or unwillingness of states to keep up with the cost of living for teachers, inadequate facilities, lousy leadership, or prioritizing away from schools and education, there is a deep sense of reality that public education in America is in real serious trouble.

Public education has left its own buildings, and the replacements that would pursue teaching have turned more often to social programs and personal pursuits, rather than academics in education.[25] At the forefront are the spoken pursuit of money[26] and the muttering lips of worker disenchantment.

Educrats cannot help but see a connection to the way funding was allocated during the competitive Race to the Top program under President Obama, and the shifts to Common Core, when states were mandated to fund a good portion of the program. Under the Trump administration there is much more local control over funding formulas.

NPR education correspondent Eric Westervelt confirms that "the Common Core and its battles, high-stakes testing, the erosion of tenure, and the evaluation of teachers by test scores, have all contributed to the crisis."[27] But how will altering a funding formula change education? Whenever the federal government incentivizes a national program that states adopt, then backs off the funding, there are bound to be economic and employment concerns down the line.[28]

Along with increasing statistical and anecdotal evidence as to the reasons teachers leave their classrooms, the conversation begins to shift to why people choose not to enter teaching in the first place. Some experts are advising students to steer clear of teaching in public education and choose private, charter, or homeschools, if they truly want a career in teaching. For example:

> Renowned author and teacher of literacy Nancie Atwell recently won the first annual $1 million Global Teacher Prize awarded by the Varkey Foundation. When she was asked by CNN whether she would advise others to be a public

school teacher, her response was that she would not. She said she would tell them to find a job in the private sector, or in an independent school instead. She spoke about how constricting the Common Core and testing have made the profession. "If you're a creative, smart young person, I don't think this is the time to go into teaching unless an independent school would suit you."[29]

DIGGING INTO THE NUMBERS

Linda Darling-Hammond and colleagues at the Learning Policy Institute published a 2016 report of the research undergirding the contemporary notions of teacher retention and teacher attrition. They estimated that annually, more than two hundred thousand teachers leave the workforce for reasons other than retirement. Other studies have determined that "young and experienced teachers display similar intent to leave the profession."[30] That equates to an average of four thousand teachers per state, understanding that the number is higher in some states than in others.

In terms of why teachers leave the workforce, LPI discovered there are "five major factors that influence a teacher's decision to enter, remain in, or leave the teaching profession."[31] Some researchers like to point to other nations and successes in education, and then point back to the United States about how the nation should emulate schools of European and Asian select nations. America is not Europe or Asia.

What the policymakers avoid is the conclusion that it is both our culture and our public education system that are primary causes and not necessarily the schools. Teachers are not leaving careers because of colleagues. There is something wrong in the system. The fact is that "teacher attrition in the United States is about twice as high as in high-achieving jurisdictions like Finland, Singapore, and Ontario, Canada."[32] However, the United States is no longer unique in its problems and other nations are now looking to us to see our solutions.

Other nations are experiencing their own serious cultural shifts, and the effects are being realized in schools and communities. This is causing uproars and is even responsible for spawning a new movement of nationalism. In parallel to the United States, teachers in other nations are also leaving their classrooms, due to increases in violence and changes in school cultures.[33] Passion turned toward violence is an ugly lesson to learn. All of this sounds familiar.

Why then are some European schools continuing to be held up to such high standards? US teachers leaving their careers behind is not as unique in the world as policymakers would like the populace to believe. Losses of autonomy and independence, greater expectations with lesser tools, and poor financial reward are universal frustrations. It is time to face the facts. People have lost interest in teaching in public schools. The question persists as to whether teacher attrition is pandemic and systemic, regardless of the motivating factors.

WHY TEACH?

There are five major factors influencing a teacher's decision as to whether to choose a career in teaching: "(1) Salaries and other compensation, (2) preparation and costs to entry, (3) hiring and personnel management, (4) induction and support for new teachers, and (5) working conditions, including school leadership, professional collaboration, and shared decision making."[34]

LPI claims that there is no silver bullet "to recruiting and retaining a 3-million person teaching workforce serving more than 50 million students across 50 states."[35] Already-suggested solutions and retreaded recommendations by the LPI and others are falling short. However, the incentive-based suggestions below comprise a nice wish list, each of which is actually meant to shape education culture as well.[36]

- Increase teachers' salaries to support a middle-class lifestyle.
- Utilize the leverage of the Every Student Succeeds Act (ESSA) to provide lower-income districts with the necessary resources to employ and retain teachers in those areas.
- Provide incentives to retain teachers, including affordable housing in areas that are cost prohibitive for teachers.
- Offer loan forgiveness programs to teachers in the areas they are most needed.
- Create and recognize cross-state portability of licensure and pensions.
- Incentivize professional development strategies and the design of schools to provide for greater cross-school collaboration.
- Offer career advancement opportunities that provide increased compensation, responsibility, and recognition.
- Provide service scholarships and loan forgiveness programs to attract prospective teachers to the fields and locations where they are needed most.
- Develop teacher residencies.
- Create local pathways into the profession, such as high school career pathways and "Grow Your Own" teacher preparation models.
- Strengthen hiring practices to ensure decisions are made as early as possible with the best candidate pool and based on the best information possible.
- Revise timelines for voluntary transfers or resignations so that hiring processes can take place as early as possible, ideally in the spring of the prior school year.

- Build training and hiring pipelines for new and veteran teachers, while monitoring and reducing teacher turnover and reducing unnecessary barriers to entry for mobile teachers.
- Invest in high-quality induction programs.
- Invest in the development of high-quality principals who work to include teachers in decision-making and foster positive school cultures.
- Survey teachers to assess the quality of the teaching and learning environment, and to guide improvements.

Even if the LPI were to gain complete fulfillment of all items on their wish list, it would still face the challenge of motivating a generation to discover that teaching is its area of passion. Unfortunately, the selling of job prospects is not enough to keep passion alive beyond the hype. Once the secret gets out that teaching is vastly different than what was sold to them, younger teachers of Gen Z will find something else to do that adds excitement and fervor.

Declining Morale

The secret is out and educators are beginning to spend more time talking about it: *Teachers are fed up with the inability to discipline students because bureaucrats have stepped in to target what they thought was targeting.* Certain folks were sure that targeting specific racial groups for inordinate discipline was placing them in line to be in prison.

The undercurrent surrounding this is immense for teachers, for at least three reasons. First, bureaucrats and social activists have gained more than a foothold in the classrooms of the nation and really have little understanding of what goes on in today's schools. Second, teachers are highly offended, although quiet about it in public, that they would be labeled as a group that is racially motivated when disciplining children in their classrooms.

A third reason is the faulty assumption that certain student demographics, because of being disciplined, are going to be the nation's next prison population. Teachers are not to blame for this, and it is offensive. Yet, what can teachers do but abide by the bureaucratic dictates in which policymakers have come to take pride? What teacher wants to feel blameworthy for sending kids to prison?

Bureaucrats should be asking the question of how many teachers have gone way out of their employment comfort zones to reach students and save them from lives of hardship. They could verify this by researching teachers that use personal money on their own students when they purchase food, supplies, and hygiene products. Teachers assist some of the neediest among us, without fanfare and to the detriment of their own finances.

The bottom line is that in schools across the land morale is down because teachers have barely any authority left to hold students accountable for their behaviors. In addition, teachers are sometimes labeled by hurtful pejoratives associated with skin color, have their motives challenged, and are even made to feel ashamed for their decisions. That type of environment of assumptions places teachers in precarious positions.

CHANGE ON THE HORIZON

In an attempt to change education culture toward teacher classroom authority and teacher morale, "U.S. Secretary of Education Betsy DeVos has rescinded guidance created by the Obama administration to ensure that students of color aren't disciplined more harshly than their peers."[37] As secretary, she heard from teacher groups around the nation of the mounting frustrations among them, by being labeled and rendered powerless by policy and unsupported by their school administrations—whose hands were also tied by the racially driven policy.

An example of this frustration is in the experience of a kindergarten teacher in Los Angeles. Erika Jones "needed to know what to do for a tantrum-throwing, book-hurling kindergartener in lieu of sending him to the principal's office . . . she discovered she'd have to teach herself a new approach to school discipline. 'For me personally, I didn't receive any training from the district.'"[38]

DeVos added,

> Every student has the right to attend school free from discrimination. They also have the right to be respected as individuals and not treated as statistics. In too many instances, though, I've heard from teachers and advocates that the previous administration's discipline guidance often led to school environments where discipline decisions were based on a student's race and where statistics became more important that the safety of students and teachers.[39]

In reversing the Obama-era guidance policy, she added, "Our decision to rescind that guidance . . . makes it clear that discipline is a matter on which classroom teachers and local school leaders deserve and need autonomy. I would encourage them to continue to implement discipline reforms that they believe will foster improved outcomes for their students."[40]

Some of the reasons given for the revocation of the Obama-era guidelines[41] include the following:

- Obama guidance policy, although nonbinding, could imply that schools were running afoul of civil rights laws, if students of color were inordinately disciplined numerically.

- The use of exclusionary discipline methods has forced teachers to reject traditional methods of discipline and continue to deal with problems in classrooms.
- Critics complained that Obama guidance was far too heavy-handed and unfair to all students.
- Educators stated that the guidelines allowed students to feel empowered, and this sometimes led to more lax classroom environments, which then led to misbehavior.

Along with local teachers associations, one of the major voices of concern involves conservative educational and political groups. For example:

> Conservative groups . . . argued that schools and districts, fearing costly civil rights investigations, imposed too many restrictions on student discipline, leading to chaotic learning environments. The discipline guidance was an act of federal overreach that led schools to remove needed discretion from teachers. . . . And some local teachers' unions have criticized their districts' discipline changes, saying they weren't adequately prepared for the changes.[42]

The reversal of the guidance policy on student discipline did not cancel the possibilities of actions that could be taken by those offended. Michael Petrilli of the Fordham Institute explains that "even without guidance, students who feel they have been discriminated against on the basis of race through a school's disciplinary decisions can still file a formal complaint with the Education Department, and the department can still investigate."[43] As Petrilli sees it, the reversal does not appear to be the real issue. "The radical departure was in 2014, when the Obama administration embraced this disparate impact approach and became very close to requiring a quota system for discipline," which reached beyond race and into "guidance related to transgender students, school diversity, sexual assault, and discipline."[44]

For now, teachers have some breathing room. When policy is exclusive for some, it naturally excludes others. Exclusiveness cuts both ways, and it challenges levels of tolerance even for the tolerant.

This is reminiscent of the "separate but equal" doctrine that emerged from the *Plessy v. Ferguson* (1896) Supreme Court case. This case was later overturned by *Brown v. Board of Education of Topeka, Kansas* (1955) when the court held that if the policy in question is one that separates (excludes), then that policy is inherently unequal (noninclusive).

The problem of teacher shortages in the United States is acute and shows no signs of going away any time in the near future. Although shortages have been observed in the past, today's shortage appears broader and deeper than anticipated. There are statistical and anecdotal reasons for these shortages, some of which can be understood by examining the (1) levels of interest in education as a major for high students and college students, (2) levels of interest in teacher education as a major as a college student, and (3) college students actually enrolling in teacher education as a major.

Tables 2.1, 2.2, and 2.3 illustrate this interest and selection. See this chapter and chapter 3 for additional information.

INTEREST IN TEACHING

During the years 2010–2014, the interest among high school students to enter education saw a downturn nationally. The percentages of students interested in teacher education fluctuated but generally fell between the years 2010–2015.[45] These are illustrated in table 2.1.

Also, UCLA's Higher Education Research Institute released national data for a ten-year window, reflecting the scope and percentages of incoming college freshmen that were likely to enroll in one of several education majors.[46] These data are reflected in table 2.2.

Beginning with the school year 2008–2009, states became serious about reporting the numbers of people enrolled in their college and university teacher education programs. In 2015, the following data were reported to the US Department of Education regarding incoming freshmen at college and their enrollment in teacher education and to train to become classroom teachers. Observe the downward trend in table 2.3.

THE SHIP IS SINKING

The 2018 Executive Summary of the National Portrait of Colleges of Education, from the American Association of Colleges for Teacher Education (AACTE), states: "The number of undergraduate education degrees awarded

Table 2.1. High school student interest in pursuing education as a major in college

School year	Number of students indicating interest in education as a major at college	Percent of students demonstrating interest in education as a major	Increase or decrease in number
2010	15,595	15%	_____
2011	13,754	13%	Decrease from 2010
2012	11,347	12%	Decrease from 2011
2013	11,089	12%	Decrease from 2012
2014	10,678	12%	Decrease from 2013
2015	10,751	12%	Increase from 2014

Table 2.2. Incoming college freshmen students expressing interest in teaching

2005	9.9%
2006	9.5%
2007	9.2%
2008	8.2%
2009	8.2%
2010	7.2%
2011	5.9%
2012	5.7%
2013	5.2%
2014	5%
2015	4.2%

The following numbers of students in a given year were on record as expressing interest in selecting education as a possible career choice.

annually peaked at almost 200,000 in the early 1970s and is less than 100,000 today."[47]

The AACTE report lists many reasons for this gradual decline of teacher enrollment over the years.

> One reason . . . is expanded opportunities available to women, who earn 80% of education degrees, in other fields. In 1970–71, 36% of all bachelor's degrees awarded to women were in education. Since then, as the total number of degrees earned by women more than doubled, the number of bachelor's degrees women earned in education dropped by almost half. In 2014–15, only 7% of all bachelor's degrees awarded to women were in education. Other factors likely affecting enrollment in teacher preparation programs include the relatively low pay of teachers and concerns about working conditions.[48]

Then there is the question about who is being prepared for what. Are apples being prepared for orange jobs? In other words, is America "overproducing certain kinds of teachers school districts aren't looking for and under-producing certain types of teachers that schools and other types of employers are desperately looking for?"[49]

That would make sense if conditions were providing evidence of that. There are "alternative teacher certification programs across the U.S. including Teach for America. But TFA, too, has seen large drops in enrollment over the past two years."[50] As the old saying goes, a person can arrange the deck chairs on the *Titanic*, but the ship is still sinking.

Table 2.3. College students enrolled in teacher education programs

2009	719,081
2010	725,518
2011	684,801
2012	623,190
2013	499,800
2014	465,536

ADDRESSING THE PROBLEMS: THE CONFERENCE ON TEACHER SHORTAGES

When many of our nation's largest states convene to hear problems associated with teacher shortages, the rest of the nation's states had better pay close attention. At the 2016 conference on California's teacher shortage, evidence was presented by state and policy experts that demonstrated the extreme nature of the state's shortage. The theme of the gathering was the "Conference on California's Emerging Teacher Shortage: New Evidence and Policy Responses." The following excerpts from California's policy experts provide evidence of the concerns about teacher shortages around the nation.

Patrick Shields

> California had faced similar issues of shortages in the 1990s, with about 10% of the teacher workforce entering the classrooms underprepared to teach the students and the contents for which they were hired. High poverty and high minority schools saw rises in warm bodies. Moving forward, fifty percent of the new hires in the early 2000s were hired unprepared and left the classroom in a few short years.[51]

Jesse Levin

> Oklahoma has a terrible shortage of teachers. There is greater demand than supply. In some content areas, especially in middle and high schools, there were higher shortages. In elementary schools, there was some surplus areas, as well as in administration. In Oklahoma, teacher mobility was examined, as some teachers moved to more affluent districts. However, the numbers of underprepared, emergency credentials rose.[52]

Massachusetts was expecting surpluses of teachers, due to enrollment declines and families moving out of the state. Yet special education, English language, and vocational tech teachers were in high demand. There are large shortages in these content areas.

Leib Sutcher

Across the nation, fewer and fewer young people are choosing to become enrolled in teacher education. In the face of demand, there are not enough teachers. Substandard credentialed teachers have increased by 63% in the last several years. These teachers are woefully underprepared. In California, in the academic year 2013–2014, one in three teachers held a credential to teach that was not earned by way of a traditional pathway, and usually hired due to demand for a "warm body."[53]

CRISIS LEVELS

In 2015, more than 40 percent of the new hires in California received credentials to teach, while being substandard in training. In single subject areas, California is in crisis shortage in the areas of math, science, and special education. In addition, large numbers of veteran teachers are teaching outside their content areas, and new hires are not choosing these subject competency areas, in which to be credentialed.[54] Observe the following:

- Teachers that are choosing to be trained and prepared are decreasing, while numbers of teachers that are substandard and credentialed are increasing.
- In 2013 and 2014, the split of special education teachers that were prepared and underprepared was about fifty-fifty.
- Some of the problems in California center on state student enrollment increases, beginning teacher disenchantment and attrition, and teacher retirements, both early and age related.
- Student-teacher ratios increased, and the changes in the ratios were caused by economics during recession.

Along with general remarks by California state-level individuals at the conference, there was also convened an expert panel. Serving on a panel discussion at the same conference was Patricia Gandara (UCLA professor), Lynn Holdheide (American Institute for Research [AIR]), and Rick Pratt (chief consultant to the California State Assembly Committee on Education), and others.[55] What follows is a brief summary of their statements and findings.

Patricia Gandara (UCLA) shared that the bilingual/English as a second language (ESL) teacher shortage is paramount, with 43 percent of California students coming from homes where English is not spoken (2.7 million students) and 85 percent speaking Spanish. California does not have bilingual education as a rule. Bilingual teachers are not being credentialed as in years past,[56] and there is a shortage of both positions and teachers in bilingual education.

Lynn Holdheide (AIR) shared that students suffer from supply and demand offsets in special education. Teachers in special education seem to leave at greater percentages and leave for many reasons. Some of these include lack of leadership, poor working conditions, role ambiguity, professional isolation, and excessive paperwork requirements.

Paperwork decreases the amount of time for instruction, and teachers want to teach. Nationally, about 60 percent of special education/disabilities students are receiving educational services in the regular classroom.[57] Estimates are that this number will rise another 10 percent over the next decade. How this will affect general education teachers is unknown.

Rick Pratt (chief consultant to the California State Assembly Committee on Education) is encouraging teachers to staff low-performing schools, so that these schools have more veteran staffs. To encourage this, and to cut into the national teacher shortage, loan forgiveness programs should be used as incentives for students to teach in high-need schools. However, because of the acuteness of the shortages in all areas of education, it might be best to offer loan forgiveness to those teachers in areas where shortages are most acute, such as special education and certain content areas in low-performing, or high-need schools.

Teachers' salaries need to rise across the board to keep pace with salary increases in individual states.[58] Under the ESSA, the Local Control Funding Formula, 95 percent of programs are funded, but because of local control, sometimes the money that is earmarked for teachers is used in another area.[59] Alternate methods can be used to add additional funds for teachers, and these should be developed.

THE SYSTEM IS BROKEN: LONG LIVE THE SYSTEM

The American public education system has multiple fractures, and these fractures do not seem to be healing. Critics would argue, "Well, let's patch over what is broken." Given all the trillions of dollars committed to public education over the years, one would think American public education would be thriving. The opposite is occurring, and it is losing steam, which is not to be confused with STEAM (science, technology, engineering, art, and mathematics), which is holding its own as a set of college majors.

This is not to say that every facet of public education is a mess. That just is not the case. But the same thing could be said about the man with one broken arm and one broken leg. Like this fellow, schools feel the breaks across the entire body of work.

ALL THINGS TO ALL STUDENTS

As with all other social programs in our nation, there are diminishing returns for the trillions spent. For example, the War on Poverty since 1964 had become a vortex, swallowing approximately an inflation-adjusted $22 trillion on antipoverty programs, as these programs grew much larger than the vision of President Lyndon Johnson and subsequent presidents ever intended.[60] In 2015, 43.1 million people lived at or below the poverty line in the United States. Compared to the more recent government data in 2017, there were 39.7 million people in poverty, and teachers in more than a few states are counted in these numbers.

An estimated 13 percent of Americans wrestle with poverty on a daily basis.[61] No one denies that poverty is a serious cultural issue. Why is it with the numbers of impoverished that come to school each day that public education is left out of the conversation about poverty. If poverty affects education, then does education affect poverty? Overcoming poverty by education is a starting point and not an endgame.

Public schools have become *all things to all people* social agencies. Students are fed, clothed, educated, counseled, and monitored daily, and many students spend more waking hours at school each day than they do at home. Truly, schools and teachers have even become surrogate families and parents for children, with para-mothers and para-fathers stepping in as needed.

There is no judgment passed on these efforts. But it is the reality of twenty-first-century education that American public schools are some of the largest antipoverty social programs in the nation—if not the largest! How does this affect those who recently entered the teaching ranks because of a desire to educate children?

Few people wish to address how our once-revered education system has turned into a social program haven, attempting to meet every need of every child within its borders—maybe because addressing serious issues and grousing about problems does little to address why little Mario needs a coat, or why Marie has to be home alone for hours as a seven-year-old. The problems that exist were years in the making. Psychologists and sociologists inform teachers on what they already know: poverty outside the schools means poverty inside the schools. Is it the responsibility of the schools or teachers to solve poverty, to educate, or both?

As was said earlier, some things can be done and some things cannot be done. One thing is certain: teachers want to teach, because teaching is their passion. Whenever social problems get in the way of their mission to teach, impassioned teachers will attempt to solve the problems. It is in their nature. But when the system itself is the problem, it becomes an insurmountable problem, and sense of purpose diminishes along with passion.

Teachers summon the will to go to work each day, hoping to educate and help students rise above mediocrity. Teachers around the nation are discovering that the external waves of change are more powerful than they can withstand. Good teachers are at a point where they wonder whether their efforts each day to stand firm and tall are worth it. Acting as a parent to students and not being able to actually parent is quite frustrating. Even with this, when it comes to working with the students, most teachers would answer that their efforts make a difference in children's lives.

It is not that good teachers have less passion toward working with students. It is the culture in which they work and live that saps them of their corporate vitality. When this happens, regardless of the generation involved, some people see it as a challenge, while others become disenchanted.

Reality Sets In

Melissa Bowers, former high school teacher, writes, "7 reasons you might not want to teach anymore." She prefaces her list with "I am not going to talk about the bone-deep exhaustion that comes from being onstage all day, or the drowning sensation that follows you home on nights and weekends when you have hundreds of papers to grade."[62] Instead, she writes about "the other things—the stuff you might only understand if you have a key to the teachers' lounge."[63] Bowers's seven-item list follows:

1. You are an "authority figure" with no real authority.
2. Your day does not resemble that of a typical white-collar professional.
3. Everyone thinks they know how to do your job. Everyone!
4. You wanted to foster imagination, not slaughter it.
5. The technology obsession is making you crazy.
6. All the entitlement and the trophies and the apathy and whatever.
7. There is no reliable way to assess who is actually good at this.[64]

Bowers continues and laments the fact that children are treated like cookies cut from the same cutters. She writes, "They are human beings, and there are thirty-five of them per class period, and they are influenced by FAR more than yesterday's vocabulary lesson." In a message to parents, Bowers exhorts them to "stop making excuses for your kids. STOP IT. Teach them to earn things, not demand things. Hold them to a higher standard. Challenge them. That way when 'I' try to challenge them, they'll know we both expect it. They'll know we are on the same team."[65]

However, what Bowers does not point out in her lament is that many of today's parents expect the teachers to acquiesce and play on the parents' teams. This is symptomatic regardless of economic station in life. Entitlement eventually gives way to expectations. The inability to make a difference is another reason teachers are losing passion for what was once their calling.

Entitled Generation

The expectation is that teachers will knuckle under and treat the students as some parents treat them at home. Confronting teachers has become a trademark of parents who have come to be known as "lawnmower parents." These are the Millennials we are talking about, and when they do not get their way on behalf of their children, they bulldoze their way forward to level the terrain. In other words, students whose parents cover for them and step in for them to avoid contending with the shortcomings of their own humanity "lack a sense of personal motivation and believe they're not good enough to accomplish things on their own because lawnmower parents have cleared and charted paths and removed obstacles."[66] When boulders impede passage, parents become the bulldozers.[67]

This type of behavior is seen especially from parents of special needs children, and not necessarily those with genuine special needs, as categories go in schools. Special needs designations today, more and more, pertain to students who chronically leave their PE equipment at home, or to those whose homework is on their computer, and on it goes. However, as one teacher speculated, "I'm not sure that the solution for every sensitive child is to remove as much struggle as possible."[68]

Middle and secondary teachers report there are dozens and dozens of 504s per daily teaching load, adding only to the impossibility of meeting the needs of all students every day. The education universe is student centered, and many of the students are parent enabled. And that is the point. Parents, "instead of preparing children for challenges, . . . mow obstacles down so kids won't experience them in the first place."[69] This is precisely what Melissa Bowers is addressing.

As Sonja Haller writes, "The problem is not a parent's willingness to help a child succeed, that's admirable and understandable. The problem comes from a parent's repeated efforts to eliminate any and all struggle so that children are ill-equipped when they grow up and life inevitably goes sideways."[70] Teachers that are restricted from challenging students to learn, and are chastised for the ways they challenge students, are not long for the classrooms. This pursuit of enablement by parents is another frustrating part of American culture that comes to school each day. It is also part of the rapid swirl that leads to teacher disenchantment and loss of dissipating passion.

CONCLUSION

What is a school to do when several of the teachers on staff are also parents and are the types of parents that were just described above? One teacher lamented her realization when she wrote, "Forget lawnmower parents—I was a lawnmower teacher."[71] Instead of allowing her students to work through struggles academically and socially, she stepped in regularly on the playground, in the classroom, and everywhere she could alleviate an issue.

In the words of Kimberley Moran, "One of my first graders had trouble with everything from opening his pencil case, to putting on his jacket. I could help him when I saw his struggle. But, I worried about how he'd do during lunch opening applesauce cups or getting ready for recess. So, I spent the beginning and end of every lunch period making sure he was okay. I stood in the cafeteria doorway or pretended I need a napkin or fork and 'happened' to walk by just as something needed opening. . . . You think being a lawnmower parent is time consuming? Try lawnmower teaching sometime."[72] Cultural impacts do come full circle and are contagious.

Tim Walker writes, "If a new teacher is vulnerable to burnout after only one or two years in the classroom, you can bet lack of administrative support, mentorship, professional development and planning are top the list of culprits."[73] Education researchers at Michigan State University "believe that teacher burnout may, to some degree, be contagious,"[74] and once the contagion spreads there are mass shortages at schools and in districts. But what are the causes of this contagion?

After surveying 171 teachers with less than four years in the classroom, as well as 289 "experienced educators who had relationships with their younger counterparts either as mentors or as colleagues,"[75] the researchers discovered "a substantial link between burnout levels in new educators and burnout among their more experienced colleagues."[76]

Those who talked with veterans with high levels of burnout were more likely also to be burned out.[77] American culture has come full circle, and new teachers are quickly being labeled as the squares. Is it any surprise as to why teachers of different grade levels, and of different numbers of years of regular teaching experience, triangulate to realize the reality of teaching is not as they perceived?

NOTES

1. Liana Loewus, "Millennial Teachers: Things to Consider in Trying to Recruit and Retain Them," *EdWeek*, December 6, 2018, https://blogs.edweek.org.

2. Freddie Cross, "Teacher Shortage Areas (TSA) Nationwide Listing 1990–1991 through 2017–2018," *US Department of Education Office of Postsecondary Education*, May 2017, https://www2.ed.gov.

3. Angela Watson, "Why I Quit My Teaching Job Mid-Year (No, It Wasn't the Testing)," *Cornerstone for Teachers*, November 22, 2012, https://thecornerstoneforteachers.com.

4. Heather Voke, *Keeping Good Teachers*, ed. Marge Scherer (Alexandria, VA: Association for Supervision and Curriculum Development, 2003), chaps. 1–2.

5. Aimee Picchi, "School's Back in Session, but Many Teachers Aren't Returning," *CBS News Money Watch*, August 23, 2018, https://www.cbsnews.com.

6. Ibid.
7. Ibid.
8. Ibid.
9. Ibid.
10. Ibid.

11. Sarah Betancourt, "Teacher Shortages Worsening in Majority of US States, Study Reveals," *Guardian*, September 6, 2018, https://www.theguardian.com.

12. Desiree Carver-Thomas and Linda Darling-Hammond, "Teacher Turnover: Why It Matters and What We Can Do about It," *Learning Policy Institute*, August 2017, https://learningpolicyinstitute.org.

13. Eric Westervelt, "Frustration. Burnout. Attrition. It's Time to Address the National Teacher Shortage," *nprEd*, September 15, 2016, https://www.npr.org.

14. Passy, "Why America's Teacher Shortage."

15. John Papay, Andrew Bacher-Hicks, Lindsay Page, et al., "America's Teacher Shortage Can't Be Solved by Hiring More Unqualified Teachers," *Washington Post*, January 9, 2018, https://www.washingtonpost.com.

16. Ibid.

17. Valerie Strauss, "The Real Reasons behind the U.S. Teacher Shortage," *Washington Post*, August 24, 2015, https://www.washingtonpost.com.

18. Eric Westervelt and Kat Lonsdorf, "What Are the Main Reasons Teachers Call It Quits?" *nprED*, October 24, 2016, https://www.npr.org.

19. Ibid.

20. Michelle Hackman and Eric Morath, "Teachers Quit Jobs at Highest Rate in Record," *Wall Street Journal*, December 28, 2018, https://www.wsj.com.

21. Passy, "Why America's Teacher Shortage."
22. Hackman and Morath, "Teachers Quit Jobs."
23. Ibid.
24. Ibid.
25. Ibid.

26. Megan Gorman, "Millennial Women Are Poised to Be the Most Financially Independent Women in History," *Forbes*, September 9, 2018, https://www.forbes.com.

27. Strauss, "Real Reasons."

28. Ernest J. Zarra III, *The Teacher Exodus: Reversing the Trend and Keeping Teachers in the Classrooms* (Lanham, MD: Rowman & Littlefield, 2018).

29. Strauss, "Real Reasons." Cf. "Nancy Atwell: CNN Special Report," *YouTube*, March 17, 2015, https://www.youtube.com.

30. Shannon V. Ryan, Nathaniel P. von der Embse, Laura L. Pendergast, et al., "Leaving the Teaching Profession: The Role of Teacher Stress and Educational Accountability Policies on Turnover Intent," *Teaching and Teacher Education* 66 (August 2017): 1–11, https://www.sciencedirect.com.

31. Anne Podolsky, Tara Kini, Joseph Bishop, et al., "Solving the Teacher Shortage: How to Attract and Retain Excellent Educators," *Learning Policy Institute*, September 15, 2016, https://learningpolicyinstitute.org.

32. Carver-Thomas and Darling-Hammond, "Teacher Turnover." Cf. Dwyer Gunn, "How States across the Country Are Dealing with Teacher Shortages," *Pacific Standard Magazine*, August 29, 2018, https://psmag.com.

33. Ernest J. Zarra III, *Assaulted: Violence in Schools and What Needs to Be Done* (Lanham, MD: Rowman & Littlefield, 2017). Cf. Zarra, *Teacher Exodus*.

34. Podolsky, Kini, Bishop, et al., "Solving the Teacher Shortage."
35. Ibid.

36. Gunn, "How States across the Country."
37. Andrew Ujifusa, "Betsy DeVos Revoked Obama Discipline Guidance Designed to Protect Students Of Color," *Education Week*, December 21, 2018, https://blogs.edweek.org.
38. Jane Meredith Adams, "Most Teachers in California Say They Need More Training in Alternatives to Suspensions, Survey Finds," EdSource, May 7, 2017, https://edsource.org.
39. Ujifusa, "Betsy DeVos."
40. Ibid.
41. Ibid.
42. Ibid.
43. Ibid.
44. Ibid.
45. Stephanie Aragon, "Teacher Shortages: What We Know," Education Commission of the States, 2016, https://www.ecs.org. Cf. "The Condition of Future Educators 2015," *ACT*, http://www.act.org.
46. Mary Ellen Flannery, "Survey: Number of Future Teachers Reaches All-Time Low," *NEA Today*, March 15, 2016, http://neatoday.org. Cf. "Freshmen Survey: Cooperative Institute Research Program (CIRP)," UCLA Higher Education Research Institute (HERI), 2016, https://heri.ucla.edu.
47. "Colleges of Education: A National Portrait," *American Association of Colleges for Teacher Education (AACTE)*, 2018, https://secure.aacte.org.
48. Ibid.
49. Eric Westervelt, "Where Have All the Teachers Gone?" *nprEd*, March 3, 2015, https://www.npr.org.
50. Ibid.
51. Patrick Shields, Learning Policy Institute, "Conference on California's Emerging Teacher Shortage: New Evidence and Policy Responses," *YouTube*, February 19, 2016, https://www.youtube.com.
52. Jesse Levin, American Institutes for Research, "Conference on California's Emerging Teacher Shortage."
53. Leib Sutcher, "Conference on California's Emerging Teacher Shortage: Statistics."
54. Ibid.
55. Patricia Gandara (UCLA), Lynn Holdheide (American Institute for Research), Rick Pratt (Policy Analysis of California Education [PACE]), "Conference on California's Emerging Teacher Shortage."
56. Ibid.
57. Ibid.
58. Podolsky, Kini, Bishop, et al., "Solving the Teacher Shortage."
59. Rick Pratt, "Policy Analysis of California Education—PACE: QEIA (Quality Education and Investment Act," *YouTube*, February 19, 2016, https://www.youtube.com.
60. Rachel Sheffield and Robert Rector, "The War on Poverty after 50 Years," Heritage Foundation, September 15, 2014, https://www.heritage.org.
61. Kayla Fontenot, Jessica Semega, and Melissa Kollar, "Income and Poverty in the United States: 2017," *US Census Bureau*, September 12, 2018, https://www.census.gov.
62. Melissa Bowers, "7 Reasons You Might Not Want to Teach Anymore," *Huffington Post*, December 6, 2017, https://www.huffingtonpost.com.
63. Ibid.
64. Ibid.
65. Ibid.
66. Sonja Haller, "Meet the Lawnmower Parent: The New Helicopter Parents of 2018," *USA Today*, September 19, 2018, https://www.usatoday.com.
67. Ernest J. Zarra III, *The Entitled Generation: Helping Teachers Teach and Reach the Minds and Hearts of Generation Z* (Lanham, MD: Rowman & Littlefield, 2017), 82, 106.
68. "Lawnmower Parents Are the New Helicopter Parents and We Are Not Here for It," *We Are Teachers*, August 30, 2018, https://www.weareteachers.com.
69. Haller, "Meet the Lawnmower Parent."
70. Ibid.

71. Kimberley Moran, "Forget Lawnmower Parents—I Was a Lawnmower Teacher," *We Are Teachers*, September 11, 2018, https://www.weareteachers.com.

72. Ibid.

73. Tim Walker, "Are New Educators Exposed to a 'Burnout Contagion' in School?" *NEA Today*, August 28, 2017, http://neatoday.org.

74. Jihyun Kim, Peter Youngs, and Kenneth Frank, "Burnout Contagion: Is It Due to Early Career Teachers' Social Networks or Organizational Exposure?" *Teaching and Teacher Education* 66 (August 2017): 250–60, https://www.sciencedirect.com.

75. Ibid.

76. Ibid.

77. Walker, "Are New Educators Exposed?"

Chapter Three

Incentivizing Mediocrity

> If we give you additional things to add to your plate as teachers, we will take something off to keep things in balance; remember we want you to work smarter, not busier.
> (common myths of education)
>
> Many schools fall far short in providing early-career educators with effective professional development, resources and preparation time. [1]

Many years ago, a professor looked at a raw and pretentious student with that dubious professorial look. The look was interpreted by the student as displeasure, and he wondered what was wrong. The professor explained his expression was a look of perplexity. The professor then followed with the challenge, "Son, why don't you go into the teaching profession?"

The student replied to the professor with his own curious look and fired back two quick questions in reply—the first of which was more of an accusation with a question mark: "Who wants to work with kids?" The second question was, "Where does one begin to even move in that direction?"

The professor laughed and drew the brief exchange to a close with his statement, "Young man, that's why we train you for the job." This exchange characterized my initial introduction into teacher training and the concept of mentoring. Those early days of mentoring were so very different from today's ideas and practices. Careers were approached differently in those days.

MENTORING AND INDUCTION

The definition for mentoring has shifted from giving advice to direct one-to-one coaching, monitoring, and teaming—all of which are now under a large umbrella of teacher induction. Regardless of the era, or the decade in which a teacher comes into the classroom, mentoring and professional development remain essential components tied to teacher longevity and success. That being said, to many outsiders, American public education is struggling to represent itself as barely mediocre.

American schools come across as trying to be all things to all students. The rumble from the inside echoes a similar refrain. Inasmuch as increasing numbers of alternatively certified teachers are hired, their training and notion of relative career longevity leave much to be desired. Has the United States now arrived at a constant, that regardless of reforms in education, the best that can be attained through aspirations and efforts is mediocrity?

Less Prepared to Teach

A growing number of today's teachers are entering the ranks with less preparation than in years past. This is challenging the status quo of teacher training and the twenty-first-century model of mentoring. In order for mentoring today to be effective, it must be attached to twenty-first-century teacher training. Consequently, both must be viewed in context of twenty-first-century teachers, and therein lies another issue. But where do we start in a system that appears headed in the wrong direction? The nation had better hurry.

The numbers of public school students are anticipated to swell to between fifty-two and fifty-three million in less than a decade.[2] Another 10–12 percent of that figure are expected to enroll in private schools. In some states the problem is presently more acute than in other states. Could it be that an unintended consequence of today's female advancements in areas other than education and teaching will put the next generation of girls in a very precarious position with less female role models as teachers in classrooms? Whoever it is had better understand the importance with which they must approach their jobs.

Rude Awakenings

Things are headed in the wrong direction for teachers when they realize what they may have signed up for is not what they experience. Can anyone blame them for leaving at midyear, or because of shifting expectations dropped on them by their administrators? One teacher recalls her point of no return:

> I remember the exact breaking point. I hadn't used our social studies books yet that year, but there was a particular passage I wanted the kids to check out as an intro to an activity. I said to the class, "Okay, when you hear the magic signal, you're going to take out your social studies books and turn to page 35." At the mention of the word *social studies*, one student burst into tears and crawled under [the] desk so he could bang his head against the floor. (Later I learned this was a reaction to social studies he'd begun having in first grade

and his previous teacher had no idea why.) Another boy murmured something under his breath, causing all the children in his vicinity to say, "Awwww, Andrew called you the B-word." Simultaneously, another child took out his social studies book but accidentally dropped it on the floor, causing the children around him to laugh. "What are you laughing at, punk? Shut the F-up!" and then punched the kid nearest him in the arm. The child who was punched did the same thing right back. The two of them sat there glaring at each other, and the other children around them were either frozen in anticipation of egging them on to fight.

Almost every child in the classroom was now either disrupting the lesson, or distracted by the disrupters. One child had her hand up asking to go to the bathroom. Another had his hand up and was pointing at the child next to him, who was gleefully ripping out pages of his social studies book. Yet another child was tapping me on my arm and asking me to repeat the page number. As I took a breath and made a decision about which fire to put out first, I heard a scuffle outside the door and a voice came over the intercom. "Lockdown, code 3 lockdown." That meant the police were pursuing a suspect in the neighborhood, and I had to cover the small window on our door and move the class away from it. It was in that moment that I knew my job was not worth the energy expenditure I had to put out every day. I wanted to teach and THAT wasn't teaching. I was maintaining some sense of order, but I wasn't teaching.[3]

The inability to teach is not what teachers spent years training for, and it certainly was not what could have possibly enticed second-career teachers to leave their previous jobs. Angela Watson, National Board Certified Teacher with many years classroom experience, as well as a K–12 instructional coach, writes five things to know if you're thinking about quitting your teaching job.

- It's not your imagination—teaching is getting harder.
- Sometimes, the school year does not get easier with time, and that's not necessarily your fault.
- You are not a bad teacher just because your job feels too hard.
- Quitting does not equal failure.
- There are lots of ways to use your talents and gifts to help children.[4]

Watson did not leave over students' assessments. However, others viewed assessment pressures and unrealistic expectations as some of the main drivers for their exodus. Still others saw very little advantage to remaining in the classroom. Another teacher, Rachel Tustin, illustrates this very point.

> In America, there are not nearly enough professional teachers to fill classrooms. Every state and school district faces teacher shortages, often in the areas of science, math, and special education. Colleges face falling enrollment in teacher education programs and more rigorous state testing requirements for

new teachers to assure that they are highly qualified to teach their subjects. Finally, once we manage to get teachers into the classroom, they are faced with the overwhelming task of trying to get their students to be successful on a variety of challenging state tests. So is tougher testing to blame for teacher shortages? Yes, but perhaps not exactly in the way you might think.[5]

Even with all of the test preparatory classes and access to smart technology in schools, the best scores our nation seems to be able to muster are often mediocre when compared to some other respected nations of the world.

DISTURBING TRENDS

The US Department of Education recently released a report from the Office of Postsecondary Education. The report included data on specialty-specific state and territory teacher shortages for several years. Special interest is placed on the years 2017–2018.[6] In general, the numbers of US states and territories that lacked teachers by category are listed in table 3.1.

THE NEEDS OF NEW TEACHERS

The needs of new teachers can be broken into three basic categories. To begin there may be teachers (1) new to their schools but not new to teaching, (2) completely new to the profession and not trained according to a traditional program, or (3) who enter the classroom with experience as a student-teacher, intern, or from a traditional or nontraditional teacher education pro-

Table 3.1. US states and territories with teacher shortages by category, 2017–2018

Special education	54
Mathematics	51
Computer science	50
Science	48
Foreign languages	48
English/language arts	36
ESL/bilingual education	34
Career technical education	32
Arts	29
Social studies	24
Pre–K	22
Health/PE	22

gram. Regardless of their entrance into teaching, new teachers have unique needs that are present. One of these needs is to be able to live and pay their monthly bills.

Teaching and Affordability

Some education advocates and teachers' groups are blaming teacher shortages on low pay.[7] There is no secret that some states pay their teachers barely enough to survive month to month. The expenditures on students in low-teacher-pay states are another issue. Low pay for teachers and low spending on students do not add up to effective education. The reason is both are living barely above the poverty line numerically. This is especially disturbing in districts that are nonwhite.[8] In fact, "the issue has caused some to leave for better paying professions, while fewer people are choosing to become teachers."[9] Who or what is going to be left if there remains heavy turnover every few years?

In an effort to understand more deeply the needs of new teachers and move beyond mediocrity, the Southern Regional Education Board (SREB) suggests an understanding of the roles of mentoring as they identify the needs of new teachers.

- *Tier 1: Low-Level Needs.* Mentors act as "information providers" to new teachers. The caution here is not to provide a multitude of procedures and how-to lists that "run the risk of inundating new teachers."[10] Basic information provides security for the mentor.
- *Tier 2: Mid-Level Needs.* Mentors act as "thought partners," as they assist new teachers in thinking through best-case scenarios, with respect to the application of particular roles and responsibilities required by the new teacher.[11] Mentees should consider this as brainstorming, or as a Socratic method of learning.
- *Tier 3: High-Level Needs.* Mentors act as "skill developers" to new teachers when they assist in crafting deeper questions about student learning, assessment outcomes, literacy focus, and differentiated instruction for special needs students.[12] This is where mentees would benefit greatly from being involved in their campus learning communities. These are also known as professional learning communities (PLCs).

Program versus the Practical

To begin, there must be clarity as to what *mentoring* and *induction* really mean. The two terms are often mistaken for one another, and the evidence of this is the fact the terms are used interchangeably. Harry Wong explains the differences:

> There is much confusion and misuse of the words *mentoring* and *induction*. The two terms are not synonymous, yet they are often used incorrectly. Induction is a process—a comprehensive, coherent, and sustained professional development process—that is organized by a school district to train, support, and retain new teachers and seamlessly progresses them into a lifelong learning program. Mentoring is an action. It is what mentors do. A mentor is a single person, whose basic function is to help a new teacher. Typically, the help is for survival, not for sustained professional learning that leads to becoming an effective teacher. Mentoring is not induction. A mentor is a component of the induction process.[13]

Along with a host of added mini-requirements for new teachers inducted into the ranks of teaching, there are variations between the lengths of the programs of induction. There is no standardized induction program, but some states administer them well and other states do not. There are also detailed requirements placed upon mentors in states. These also vary state to state. A brief summary of five select induction program lengths, including mentoring requirements, is presented in table 3.2.[14]

One of the most important justifications for an induction program that includes sustained mentoring is the number of teachers joining the ranks without all of the necessary training required for success on their first days on the job. As a result, it is important to address policy considerations for those seeking alternative certifications and the implications this certification may have on the needs of teachers.

Professional development can also play a critical role in induction, in the process of informing newer teachers. But among all of these considerations, there must emerge more than moderate, or tolerable outcomes. Mediocrity may be the zenith for education.

TEACHERS-IN-TRAINING ASSESSMENTS

There are those who claim the teacher preparatory summative assessments, taken by prospective teachers, are themselves to blame for some of the nation's teacher shortage. In fact, the allegations run the gamut from (1) the assessments do not test what teachers will be teaching, to (2) one-size-fits-all assessments across all state and territories is no longer an accurate method of measuring new teachers, and (3) the assessments are cash cows for the Educational Testing Service (ETS)—the writers and overseers of the program—and (4) the assessments are racist.

Regardless of the outcry and the criticism, the teacher assessments remain the general requirements of states for people who intend to become teachers. Among other local or state assessments, the big three are

- Praxis Core exams,

Table 3.2. Select states with induction and mentoring requirements

State	Induction program length	Mentoring and/or professional development	Mentor requirements
Ohio	4 years	• Mentoring • Assessment • Counseling	• Teacher certification • 5-year professional license • Completion of mentoring program
North Carolina	3 years	• Formal orientation • Mentoring • Professional development	• Demonstrated record of success • Local criteria
Illinois	2 years	• Mentoring • Professional development • Counseling	• Demonstrated effective teaching practice • Strong intra- and inter-personal skills • Demonstrated knowledge of pedagogy and diverse learning needs
New Jersey	1 year	• Professional development • Orientation • Mentoring	• Teacher certification • 3 years teaching experience and has taught full time for 2 of the last 5 years • Demonstrated record of success in the classroom • Complete mentor program
New York	1 year	• Mentoring • Local programs negotiated locally	• Teacher certification • Completes district selection process

- State pedagogy exams, and
- Content portions of Praxis, specifically the level expected for licensure.

Among other criticisms, some argue that the Praxis is a biased test, meant to keep teachers of color out of the profession. After all, the pass rates of Caucasians who take the test for the first time are generally higher than other demographic groups. For example, "in 2015, the *New York Times* reported a first time pass rate of 55% for Caucasian test-takers on the new math test, and the pass rates were significantly less for Hispanic and African American test takers."[15]

The question of bias always seems to emerge when there are disparities in assessments across racial groups. Nearly one-half of Caucasians take the Praxis and do not pass. No one should ever suggest that people taking the assessments had mediocre public school educations. In all candor, as accusations fly, they add up to just another reason that things are headed in the wrong direction in twenty-first-century American education.[16]

There is always more to the story of assessment than test writers and implicit bias. There are issues of preparation, study habits, ability levels, personal finances, and the fact that not everyone is cut out to teach. Then there's the tests themselves, and even the costs of test-prep classes and for signing up to take one or more tests may be contributing factors "deterring college students and graduates from entering the profession."[17]

The bottom line is that "testing is a double-edged sword driving the teacher shortage in America. One the one hand, we are making it harder to get teachers into the classroom in the first place. Aspiring teachers must pass . . . challenging, rigorous tests to achieve certification. The tests are costly to take and most boast less-than-inspiring pass rates."[18]

Efforts to counter poor Praxis results have led to people being hired under emergency credentials, as long as they are able to pass a district-acceptable assessment, which is usually written at an eighth-grade level. The Praxis assessment is becoming a hurdle that may soon be removed from the race toward becoming a teacher. Dropping regulations is unfair to those who played by the rules previously and does little to bolster confidence in public education with communities.

MENTORING AND EXPECTATIONS

Mentors have their plates full of work. New teachers do not necessarily have a thorough understanding of today's students. Mentors can help to expedite this understanding. A good mentor can also bring the real world of education into perspective and showcase its relevance in practical ways to benefit the teacher and the students.

Knowing how to apply mentoring to bring teachers up to speed is the expedient goal of mentoring. New teachers are desperate for education that includes understanding of child development, managing and teaching special needs students, general classroom management strategies, building of appropriate relationships with children, strategic pedagogy, and accurate assessment development.

Aside from the obvious reasons that training teachers and mentoring them is so very important, there is another layer of importance to consider. The public has expectations that new teachers should somehow demonstrate veteran temperament, as well as the abilities to perform veteran skill sets.

Certainly, these are unreasonable expectations placed upon newer teachers, especially those coming from nontraditional programs, online programs, or from the workforce with no prior teaching experience. Nevertheless, these are the expectations, and mediocrity is not assumed. No parents want to write off an entire year of their child's education.

Nearly one-fourth of new teachers do not last throughout their first five years of teaching. "Staff attrition costs districts billions of dollars, contributes to low teacher morale, and disrupts student learning."[19] One of the factors for the rate of attrition is that teachers experience a lack of administrative and instructional support.[20] Teaching is quite difficult, despite how easy some teachers make it look. For example:

> That's why most mentoring programs for new teachers focus on skill-related goals, such as improving instructional delivery and applying feedback. But the ins and outs of being a teacher are hard too. Becoming a teacher can come with emotional challenges. New teachers want assurance that the professional and personal challenges they are experiencing are normal. Supporting new teachers needs to be more than just sharing information, providing instructional coaching and designing professional development. It also needs to come in the forms of empathy, perspective and advice. When mentors work on professional growth goals without probing a teacher's mindset or emotional health, skill development can become distracting, stressful and even counterproductive.[21]

RETHINKING MENTORING

Mentoring may not be enough to keep all teachers in their classrooms, or offer proper incentives to recruit new teachers to fill certain employment shortages. Any professional that acts less like one with each passing year only increases the downward movement. The Southern Regional Education Board (SREB), which represents sixteen southern states, seems to understand this.

The SREB produced a policy document on the mentoring of new teachers. The document is categorized into three sections that ask educators to "(1) Rethink program elements that affect mentors, (2) Address challenges that new teachers really face, and (3) Use a tiered process to respond to needs."[22] This is a nice step for organizations wishing to reexamine mentoring.

In section 1 of the SREB document on mentoring, there are two program elements. The first element addresses the selection of mentors, and element 2 is a type of professional development for mentors, as they seek to continue to grow in their mentorship. Currently, twenty-nine states have laws or rules for the definition and selection of mentors who are hired to work with new teachers. These states seem to have little sense about cross-state consistency of policy.

For example, regulations tie mentoring to teacher inductions. The regulations vary in these twenty-nine states. Some of the characteristics of these programs are illustrated below in select states.

- Twenty-nine of the fifty states require induction or mentoring for beginning teachers.
- Eleven of the twenty-nine require mentoring only during first years in the classroom.
- Fifteen states require mentoring for all first- and second-year teachers.
- Six states—California, Connecticut, Iowa, Maine, Missouri, and Vermont—require induction for all first- and second-year teachers.
- Nine states require mentoring that is greater than two years.
- Ohio requires a four-year-long program.
- Delaware, Hawaii, Louisiana, Maryland, Massachusetts, Michigan, North Carolina, and Utah require mentoring for three years.
- Louisiana is inconsistent in the application of any induction and mentoring policy.
- Three other states require new teacher mentoring but avoid stating a minimum.
- Colorado allows school districts to determine how long new teachers should be mentored, and it can run up to three years.
- Rhode Island requires school district plans to include some process for mentoring new teachers.
- Wisconsin requires school districts to provide qualified mentors for beginning teachers for a period that may be for less than five years.
- Seven states do not require mentoring for all beginning teachers but do require it for certain new teachers.
- Four states (Alabama, Florida, Mississippi, and Tennessee) require mentoring only for those teachers who possess alternative certification.
- Alaska requires mentoring for teachers with a specific subject-matter expert but limited certificate.
- Nevada requires mentoring for teachers with special qualifications licenses.

- North Dakota requires mentoring for teachers who seek a Teaching Alternative Flexibility Endorsement (TAFE).
- The Alaska Department of Education and Early Development partnered with the University of Alaska to create the Alaska Statewide Mentor Project (ASMP).[23]

Cohorts, residencies, emergency credentials, provisional certificates, life experience credits, and even veteran status are enough, in many states, to stand in front of a classroom and begin teaching.[24] The rethinking of mentoring leads to a conclusion that states work from different practical applications of their programs, and some states take it more seriously than others.

Specifically, today's mentoring necessitates professional development of a person to stand ready to deal with the challenges of teaching. Some of the challenges are cross-cultural and intercontextual. Other challenges are unique to states and their districts. Indeed, the challenges are many, and states must question whether their policy exacerbates the attrition of teachers from the classrooms.

One conclusion is inescapable. There is so much confusion within and across states in this new age of teacher shortages, as each state struggles to acquire enough teachers to staff their schools. This confusion has led to a messy and almost incomprehensible mash-up of mediocre policies. Mentoring within this mess only makes things messier. Florida is a prime example of a teacher attrition mess.

This concern over mentoring of teachers is at such a critical stage for Florida that "nearly 40% of new teachers in Florida leave their jobs within five years, according to state records—a rate 15 to 20 percent higher than the national average."[25] All of this is coming from a state that requires mentoring for primarily those who are hired to teach with alternative certification. But mentoring has come under greater scrutiny in Florida and in other states.

The literature is clear and bolstered by teacher anecdotes. Mentoring is so very important for new teachers, even in Florida. It is common knowledge that good mentoring can make or break a young teacher's career. How then can something so important to careers be so ineffective toward its goals? In light of this, the Brevard Federation of Teachers (BFT), along with a few teachers, were honored with a grant, which the BFT used to invest in "a teacher-led, union-run orientation program," which established "meaningful mentorships between new and veteran teachers."[26]

The way the program was set up involved both mentors and mentees being granted funded iPads. They both used the iPads "to record each other in the classroom,"[27] and then were able to sit together to analyze exactly what each other saw throughout the instruction they recorded. The support the mentees felt was noteworthy, and its success anticipates mirroring the national data that find that nine out of ten first teachers assigned mentors return to their classrooms.

But feeling appreciated does not necessarily translate to being supported toward career longevity. States like Florida understand that iPads won't solve the larger issues associated with teacher attrition in their states, but they might "feel" better about having to deal with them.

REAL ALTERNATIVES?

The following are some examples of the impacts of teacher's shortages on states and districts and their modifications to address these impacts. States are being forced to come up with plans, or "a varied roadmap,"[28] to staff their schools. Some of these include (1) hiring more and more teachers with no teaching experience—or young people who have graduated from college with a degree not in education; and (2) hiring what are referred to as content specialists, or someone who is "looking to move into teaching" and leave another career behind.[29] In the middle of all of the planning is the issue of finances.

Teach for America

The program Teach for America (TFA), which is nearly three decades old, began as "a radical teacher recruitment and preparation model, placing high-achieving college graduates without formal education training into short-term jobs in low-income communities."[30] TFA is found in fifty-one communities across the United States.[31] Another alternative program is Teach for All, and its focus is global.[32] The program has always come with a promise of money at the end of a person's contract with TFA.

As with all other alternative education programs, there are issues to face when the traditional classroom teachers' unions and associations mobilize on behalf of their contractual demands. Teachers' associations that vote to strike place TFA teachers in precarious spots. TFA teachers are caught in the middle over what to do. Do they support teachers' groups they may have joined, or do they remain with nonunion TFA government workers and cross picket lines?[33] When teachers go out on strike, the real losers are the students.

The concerns and risks are great, given financial cash perquisites that could be forfeited by TFA employees who choose to support a teachers' union strike. An alternative program that places teachers in such middle positions is not the best tool for teacher recruitment. However, TFA has been known to be an adversary to traditional teacher training institutions. That old axiom that necessity is the mother of invention could today be translated as necessity is the parent of hostility and exasperation.

Bob Bruno, a professor of labor and employment at the University of Illinois, believes that Teach for America intentionally allows teachers to skip the traditional teacher training process. He claims, the TFA program was designed "in a way that made it immediately hostile to teachers. Teachers who've gone through teacher colleges, who did apprentice programs and student teaching programs, the TFA model thumbs its nose at all of that."[34] Mediocrity and antagonism are not necessarily compatible, but sometimes they seem relatable.

THE CHASE IS ON

At Boise State University's College of Education, "90% of graduates move on to jobs in Idaho schools. The colleges are producing new teachers. . . . The problem comes a couple of years later, when rural districts try to hang on to teachers with some experience."[35] Actually, the problem shows up in year 1 when the teachers are paid so poorly that they have to take second jobs just to make ends meet.

In Arizona, "public schools statewide are struggling to fill vacancies as they attract fewer new teachers and more experienced ones retire or leave the profession for more lucrative careers. Teachers say low pay, long workdays, a lack of professional respect and opportunities elsewhere are luring them away from a field they love."[36]

In 2017, and in to 2018, according to the Arizona Department of Education

> more than 1,000 teachers in more than 120 Arizona school districts and charter schools have been certified to teach tens of thousands of students through a certificate that requires no formal education training. The number of these certificates—called Emergency Teaching Certificates—eclipsed the 789 certificates issued for 2016 school year. . . . The certificates require at least a bachelor's degree but allow the applicant to bypass nearly every other state certification requirement put in place to ensure teachers are qualified to lead a classroom.[37]

Educators in Arizona said the rate of Emergency Teaching Certificates issued this year is symptomatic of the state's worsening teacher crisis.[38] Moreover,

> in June 2017, *The Republic* . . . found 22 percent of 46,000 teachers last school year lacked the full qualifications of a standard certificate. That analysis . . . also found that nearly 2,000 teachers last year (2016) had not completed formal teacher training. More than 40 teachers lacked college degrees . . . teachers continue to enter and leave Arizona's public education system at an alarming rate, citing low pay, low support, stressful working conditions and diminished respect.[39]

The morale for teachers is so low in Arizona, when asked "whether they would recommend the profession to their children, 19 percent answered yes, 56 percent said no and 25 percent were unsure. Of those who said they would not, 94 percent cited 'substandard pay,' and 73 percent mentioned declining parental support, and 64 percent cited lack of community support."[40]

Despite the promises and meager efforts of states to raise the salaries of teachers, colleges and universities face additional dilemmas in training teachers. In Arizona, the UA College of Education saw enrollment dip by nearly 20 percent between 2009 . . . and 2013 . . . nearly half of those are out-of-state students who tend to leave Arizona after graduation, compounding the teacher shortage.[41]

DO TEACHERS WANT TO WORK IN TWENTY-FIRST CENTURY PUBLIC SCHOOLS?

There are some deep-seated concerns held by veteran teachers that new teachers are going to inherit. Teachers believe they are working during a very restrictive time and that their autonomy is challenged more today by required programs and curriculum. Throughout the decision-making processes for their schools, teacher autonomy is at all-time lows. Frustrations rise when states decide on education issues without ever having gained serious education input.

For example, along with programs aimed at curbing student detentions and expulsions, especially among middle and high school students, states are mandating reductions in formal discipline write-ups. In other words, official reports are decreasing, and along with these mandates, strict guidelines are imposed regarding how discipline is handled, especially in cases that would have been sent to the office for similar behaviors in the past.[42]

Schools' discipline policies must be adjusted to the culture in which the school is situated. In high-crime areas, or in single-parent homes, across neighborhoods of violence and addiction, for example, the pipeline-to-prison mantra becomes more understandable. That is, students from these types of backgrounds are more susceptible to be in prison one day if they are not kept in school.

It is completely unacceptable to tie discipline to races of students in any way. The reality is that all children exhibit certain behaviors, regardless of their economics and family culture. A teacher that uses discipline as a threat to a student from a broken home, where emotional or physical abuse is commonplace, might be missing the forest for the trees, especially in dealing with circumstances arising from intergenerational trauma.

However, all things must be balanced with the understanding that teachers are in the classrooms at a time when disrespect is pervasive and coarse language is virtually unpunishable. Welcome to the new world of restorative justice (RJ). Not everyone is accepting of this new policy.

Nevertheless, the application of RJ is seeing some short-term benefits in reducing poor behaviors and preventing some crime among students of color.[43] Whether it is Common Core, social emotional learning (SEL), or restorative justice, the question is, should such programs be forced into implementation in all districts in every state?

There is no secret that blatant disrespect and verbal abuse is prevalent among students. Social media—along with some forms of online bullying—has not helped to curb this reality. When students' learning diminishes, their behaviors may become problematic and teachers burn out more quickly. What happens when despite all the traditional training and preparation a teacher undergoes, students do not comply or even care to achieve? When students are in this mode, it may be quite likely that students are already in some sort of self-imposed troublesome pipelines.

Teachers then need to be trained in strategies of changing states of mind and daily growth mindset. When it comes to restorative justice, even if there is frustration over the program, it would be most helpful for teachers at least to have been trained in it,[44] even as the jury is out on its overall effectiveness to accomplish its stated goals.[45]

ALTERNATIVE PATHWAYS TO CERTIFICATION

Policy considerations are important when dealing with alternative certifications for those seeking to teach, regardless of the state. There is a growing trend by states and school districts to license or certify teachers in ways that are meant initially to close the attrition gap. The questions of teacher quality and career longevity then become foremost. In reality, some of the more practical policy considerations suggested to achieve hiring goals cannot escape their alignment with alternative certification.

- Reduce financial barriers to enter alternative programs through stipends and tuition reductions.[46]
- Reward the merit of alternative teacher candidates by waiving course work and assessments, or allowing them to test out of coursework requirements.[47]
- Provide practical and relevant teacher development for alternatively certified teachers, during the first year of the teaching. This could be accomplished by partnering with a college or developing district-level mentoring that could be used immediately in the classrooms.[48]
- Analyze similar states' requirements for alternative certification, and find those that best suit the state in question for implementation.

- Improvise on recruiting from established professions outside of education, by appealing to those seeking to make a midcareer change and offer *recruit-friendly* options for them to make the change and to attain their goals.
- Work with one or more colleges to develop on-the-job teaching training modules and professional development that maximize practicality and relevance for both elementary and secondary teachers needing support. Allow both veteran and newer teachers to earn credits on the salary schedule for taking modules via a professional development academy.[49]
- Continue to press for ways to place newly trained teachers in high-need schools, by petitioning the state to provide stipend funding, or bonuses for alternatively trained teachers to commit to teaching for a determined period of time. Again, surveys of the states would help to gain perspective on the variations of such programs and their requirements.[50]

At this juncture, two aspects of certification deserve closer examinations: (1) general categories of state certification methods and (2) pathway variations across states. The first is expanded as a list of categories that encapsulate teachers seeking certification to work in America's public schools. Most teachers hired would probably be found within one of these categories.

The second list is a detailed breakdown of alternative pathways for teacher certification across most states. In all likelihood, veteran teachers and new teachers will find that one or more of these pathways is relevant to them personally. Both the categories and the pathways are taken seriously as hiring teachers from outside education gains momentum nationally.

General Categories of State Certification Methods

- Traditional teacher education program, face-to-face
- Nontraditional teacher education, online program
- Traditional and nontraditional blended teacher education program
- Alternative certification program with added state requirements
- Emergency or temporary certification program with no education experience

Pathway Variations across States

Traditional

- Traditional four- or five-year state teacher education program with master's degree and state certification
- Traditional five-year state teacher education program with state certification

- Traditional four-year state teacher education program with state certification

Modified Traditional

- Modified traditional teacher education program, hybrid cohorts with state certification

Nontraditional

- Nontraditional/traditional online teacher education program with state certification
- Nontraditional teacher education program through assessment and limited state certifications
- Nontraditional alternative teacher licensure with BA and enrollment in traditional program
- Nontraditional alternative teacher licensure with BA and enrollment in traditional program, teaching outside of content area or area of expertise
- Nontraditional district-approved emergency teacher licensure with BA
- Nontraditional district-approved emergency teacher licensure hired as intern before college graduation
- Nontraditional district-approved emergency temporary licensure as long-term substitute
- Nontraditional district-approved substitute emergency licensure

The fact is that there are more pathways available today for people to become teachers than in recent memory, and these pathways bring with them some anxieties. Most of the pathways are incentivized by dropping regulations. However, that does not mandate better education for students. Since the demand for teachers remains extremely high, states and districts are willing to sacrifice some of the training and even the quality of the persons they hire. They instead opt for front-end guarantees that to maintain their position, these teachers must comply with a plan to earn full state certification. Yes, the demand for teachers is extremely high, but the training of the incoming supply has never been more important. What is tolerable and adequate is the acquiescence toward mediocrity.

DEVELOPING A MENTORING PROGRAM FOR THE EMERGING TEACHERS

Now with all of the innovative ways a person can become a teacher, it is incumbent upon educators to develop a newer mentoring model—one that fits the current needs of the emerging teachers and raises their educational

IQ. It is important to ask what this new mentoring program would look like and how it would be implemented. Along with face-to-face mentoring, any new model must consider online and distance components in its plan. These are the preferred ways that Gen Z teachers-in-training choose to learn.

The late 1990s were an interesting time in public education. In some states there were more teachers than there were openings. Those in midcareer at the time can recall being asked to change grade levels, or to take on a new teacher as a mentor. During those days, school districts were "working with teacher associations, universities, and others to establish mentoring programs to help beginning teachers, veteran teachers in new assignments, and teachers in need of remedial aid to build up to the difficult climbs with the assistance of a guide."[51]

Thus, the nation was undergoing a paradigm shift and many still in the classrooms today are the result of that new period of mentoring. There is another shift under way. This shift is very different and will affect both the students and the teachers that occupy the same classroom yet are from the same generation.

Incentive to Mentor

The intention is that mentors are to be exemplars at every level, both professionally and personally, and consistent in character. Some states understand the role of the mentor differently than others. A few states have incentives in place to attract mentors and develop new ones.

Some of these incentives include reduced teaching loads, to be available during the day for teachers in need. There are also stipends for mentors in many districts, along with continued professional development in mentor training. Some districts are trying out new ideas as incentives to retain teachers. Becoming a mentor is a nice tactic.

Illinois, Arizona, and New York are trying out some unusual ideas to see whether these ideas may be the incentives needed to attract teachers to their states and cities. In Pekin, Illinois, Pekin Community High School is helping teachers with "affordable and convenient child care" directly at the school.[52] The onsite childcare facility charges teachers just $100 per week.[53]

The public schools of Nashville, Tennessee, opened up a wellness center—a free gym for teachers and their dependents, although other personnel may also use it.[54] Teacher wellness and a free gym membership is highly enticing to some teachers. Mentoring is taking on new forms. Other cities such as Vail, Arizona, and Rochester, New York, are offering teachers tiny homes in which to reside and paid sabbaticals, respectively.[55]

Anyone interested in securing the role of mentor should check in advance with districts at the time of application and interview. The ultimate hope for any mentor is that "in due time the profession as a whole will be able to tackle the Everests of the educational landscape."[56] The value of good mentoring is of incredible value to the mentors, the mentees, and the students.

Districts like those in Arizona, Illinois, New York, and Tennessee are willing to reach out and offer a very different form of mentoring—one that focuses on the actual person's family and personal wellness, and not just the work they perform. These districts, and others, are demonstrating creativity along with their desperation for new teachers.

Good Mentoring

A good mentoring program will be part of a good teacher induction process. Good mentoring also occurs with the hiring of good mentors. The benefits of these as a unit give schools the best chances to retain good teachers. Since Gen Z are mostly a groupthink generation, there is hope in that which benefits all. Harry Wong agrees:

> Good teachers know that they must have colleagues who have similar standards and expectations. Accomplished teachers are more likely to choose to work in schools when there will be a "critical mass" of like-minded colleagues who share their commitment to student achievement and where the principal is the key to establishing this commitment to teacher improvement and student achievement. The bottom line is good teachers make the difference. Trained teachers are effective teachers. Districts that provide structured, sustained training for their teachers achieve what every school district seeks to achieve—improving student learning.[57]

More recently and, out of necessity, states have had to become more creative in their mentoring of new teachers. The state of Virginia, like other states, recognizes this important time in history and the subsequent value of effective mentoring. In one of its landmark documents, there are remnants of this recognition.

> Mentor programs help beginning teachers make a successful transition into teaching by relying on the expertise of veterans to provide a clinical, real-world training process. Districts that provide effective support attract the most capable candidates, who remain on the job and improve student performance. New teachers who are mentored receive higher ratings from their principals, develop better planning skills, handle discipline problems more effectively, conduct more productive classroom discussion, and remain in classrooms. . . . Veteran teachers who serve as mentors report increased professional revitalization, less isolation, greater recognition, and a belief that they impact the profession more than teachers who are not involved in mentoring new professionals.[58]

There is a lot of truth in the statement that continued mentoring helps to rekindle the passion for veteran teachers and also helps to provide the necessary foundations for newer teachers. Passion is a quality that distinguishes many teachers from their colleagues. Mentors pass along not only tips and insights but also a portion of themselves as people, through their mentoring. In order to ensure this type of development, good mentors are necessary. However, with rates of attrition as they are, is it still possible to bring public school teachers into the classrooms in sufficient numbers?

A report by the National Education Association Foundation (NEAF) identified four general categories of qualities that characterize good mentors. These qualities have proven to be essential by those with whom they work. The four categories of qualities are (1) attitude and character, (2) professional competence and experience, (3) communication skills, and (4) interpersonal skills.

Generally, those teachers who are selected as mentors should be role models for teachers, be resilient, flexible, and open-minded, as well as collegial, and use everyone's time wisely. Among others things, there is to be a trusting and approachable relationship developed between mentor and mentee, and an excellent grasp on content, pedagogy, and classroom management.[59]

PUBLIC EDUCATION AS A NEW AMERICAN FACTORY

Public education in America seems to be repeating itself. In some ways the system is in a throwback mode. This repetition is reminiscent of a previous century in both policy and practice. Welcome to the new American factory generation.

There is little mentoring of relationships on factory assembly lines. Making widgets every day is done by the same process and with the same requirements. One of the more frustrating downsides for teacher educators is that training teachers has become like a cookie-cutter process, complete with assessments of the one-size-for-all variety that have to be passed. This sounds like the oft-repeated dirge-like commands of take out your math books or work on your iPads for thirty minutes—with each repeated at the same time every day.

Finding good mentors from within a batch of good teachers is not accomplished by a half-baked process. There is something terribly off-center when schools look and act like factories. Some people are shying away from a career in teaching because the system is not friendly to their career aspirations.

In fact, it would be farfetched to consider that those coming to teaching from another career are doing so to escape the very doldrums of their own quasi-factory model. Imagine their surprise when they figure out that they have exchanged one factory model for another. The bottom line is that teachers must comply and are expected to demonstrate alacrity and be friendly to a system that is not friendly to them.

The truth is that teaching should be neither an obtuse nor an arcane form of science. Likewise, teaching should not be either scripted or formulaic. Teaching is more than science; it is an art, a craft, and highly relational. Furthermore, even though it feels like it, actual teaching is nothing like a conveyor belt run by bells and numbers.

Building people cannot be process constricted. Yet, this is where so many policymakers, as well as many in politics, desire public education to be found. So, when bureaucrats begin to talk about aligning all of this, or making certain everyone has the same hoops though which to jump, these efforts are reminiscent of the approach that was highly criticized in the past for resembling an assembly line.

MOVING TOWARD SOCIALISM?

There are no appropriate labels to be applied to all American students, and neither should there be expected one series of outcomes on assessments. For example, when government at the federal level thinks one particular change for schools is good for one group, it soon becomes mandated for all groups. Therefore, if a student has to be assessed then all students have to be assessed. Veteran educators have seen their fair shares of these actions.

Bureaucrats have not yet learned from recent dealings with Race to the Top, Common Core, and the Every Student Succeeds Act (ESSA). Major changes such as these are usually brought to bear from within politics, and someone gets the proverbial kudo. These changes are often the results of bureaucratic power plays, or policy driven by lawsuits by one or more groups that think on behalf of everyone else.

No Competition Allowed?

Few can argue that high-stakes testing and Common Core State Standards Assessments were not one-size-fits-all efforts. Fewer still can argue that under a previous administration, changes in social policy forced people to comply with new lifestyles, even against their personal beliefs. The mandate to increase graduation rates and a near guarantee that all will go to college are just a couple of the current power plays that appear much like socialism.

Graduation rates are increasing, yet the levels of reading and work production are coming in at lower rates lower than in previous generations.[60] Demand for teachers is extremely high, and the supply of teachers is desperately low. In a competitive market, the greater the demand the higher the wages, usually. However, teachers are not allowed to compete with each other.

Unions and associations bargain for wages and benefits, but economic principles of supply and demand are tossed out when it comes to schooling and funding public education. The mantra is *if one gets a raise, everyone gets a raise*. Money is being taken by extremely high taxes and given to communities in states with lower socioeconomic status (SES). Even the minutes of the day are worked out to the second.

Teachers Near Poverty Level

But why shouldn't some teachers be paid more? The reason is that it is not deemed fair to the rest of the workers. There is no way to objectivize efforts. Besides, what is in place to stop teachers from cheating? Actually, one of the only measures that could bring additional salaries to teachers is coming back alive the next year. When they do return, teachers are then rewarded with another year of credit and a possible salary schedule increase.

Good teachers cannot be paid more for their goodness, and bad teachers cannot have money removed for their poor teaching. Teachers can be paid more if they take on additional titles and jobs in addition to their teaching. Job titles and not job efforts are the impetus for increased salaries.

The fact is clear that "despite the evidence that salaries influence teacher recruitment and retention, a teacher's salary in much of the United States is too low to support a middle-class existence. A recent study from the Center for American Progress, for example, found that, in 30 states, midcareer teachers who head families of four or more are eligible for government subsidies, such as subsidized children's health insurance or free or reduced-price school meals."[61] Is this the mediocrity that bureaucrats seek, all while many of them send their own children to private schools, or by purchasing access to elite schools by donations?[62]

On the whole, the culture of public education is not about monetary packages and incentives for teachers. The fact is that the American public education system is more concerned about equality of outcomes over opportunities. Of course, there is no such thing as true democracy, pure capitalism, or even completely socialist-type systems, either in government or in education.

Nevertheless, there are clear indications that public education is often found in the socialist camp when it comes to the ways students are trained to think in schools, as well as how most employees are compensated. For example, public schools train students by masses in programs that are meant to be good for the whole. The common good of the school means that no one person is more important than another.

Realistically, this philosophy breaks down involving schools when parents fill the stands and bleachers at games where their children are competing. Suddenly, schools jettison the socialist model. Winning over the other teams is the ultimate measure of success. Competition produces winners and losers. If school and club sports were like classrooms, then everyone would play in every game, and every game would end in a tie, so as not to hurt someone else's self-esteem. Of course, this is absurd.

Athletes and parents want to win. In fact, socialists also want to win, because there is power in winning. Even the socialist politicians who are serving in the US Senate and the House of Representatives understand their voice is greater than the average citizen. Over time it is another system to which they are exposed. Eventually their practices demonstrate how quickly they veer from their core principles.

EQUALITY OF OUTCOMES

Today, the message is everyone graduates. This philosophy does little for the learning or quality of the product graduated. The outcome is what is important, and it is virtually guaranteed. Teachers are tired of being the lone voice on behalf of a student who needs to be retained or placed in a specific program outside the conventional class.

If students cannot rise to the occasion by competing, then barriers are removed and standards are reduced and requirements revised. Everyone has to graduate to show equity in the system. If there was ever any doubt about the impact of socialism in education, the evidence is in *social promotions*.

A high school diploma has become the certificate everyone gets to demonstrate educational mediocrity. Hearkening back to the assembly line, distributing diplomas is a demonstration of controlled outcomes, with less concern about quality of the product. Was the group Pink Floyd really that far off with their music video "The Wall"?

CONCLUSION

Many public school students who are currently in need of remedial classes and cannot read above the fourth-grade level are still being graduated. In the name of racial, ethnic, and socioeconomic equity, quality takes a hit. Students in line to graduate in the United States are endlessly being compared to students from other nations. Comparatively, the United States is woefully and miserably behind other nations in many academic subjects.[63] But this is all right. Our nation's students are graduating at record numbers.

Inferior products turn out to be lesser-rans and often come up short on a global scale. Every product must make it to the assembly finish line, even if it means sacrificing quality of other products being manufactured. Herein lies a major problem with the socialist education model. Despite making everything appear fair for everyone, there are always winners and losers, and these are often decided by those who are in the winning seats. What is fair for the people is not considered with the same fairness from the perspectives of the bureaucrats calling the shots.

Providing equity by empowerment does little to reduce the possibility that those previously kept down will not then take power and practice the same thing. So, what is the implication of all of this for American education? Tyranny at any level must be rejected.

As Lord Acton, the British aristocrat once stated, "Great men are almost always bad men, even when they exercise influence and not authority. . . . Everybody likes to get as much power as circumstances allow, and nobody will vote for a self-denying ordinance."[64]

In conclusion, for all the discussion and all the idealism, mentoring teachers today is as much about mentoring them into a mediocre system as it is about keeping them in line with the hierarchy's mandates. The best-trained athlete who is trained by mediocre coaches and placed on a mediocre team that is short on players cannot expect the best of outcomes.

If excellence breeds excellence, what then does mediocrity breed? Could anyone still wonder why Gen Z does not carry deep passion for a career in education and wants very little to do with teaching in American public schools?

NOTES

1. Tim Walker, "Are New Educators Exposed to a 'Burnout Contagion' in School?" *NEA Today*, August 28, 2017, http://neatoday.org.
2. Jacob Passy, "Why America's Teacher Shortage Is Going to Get Worse," *New York Post*, February 14, 2018, https://nypost.com.
3. Angela Watson, "Why I Quit My Teaching Job Mid-Year (No, It Wasn't the Testing)," *Cornerstone for Teachers*, November 22, 2012, https://thecornerstoneforteachers.com.
4. Ibid.
5. Rachel Tustin, "Are Tougher Tests the Reason for the U.S. Teacher Shortage?" *Study.com*, September 2018, https://study.com; Cf. Valerie Strauss, "Teacher Shortages Affecting Every State as 2017–18 School Year Begins," *Washington Post*, August 28, 2017, https://www.washingtonpost.com.
6. Freddie Cross, "Teacher Shortage Areas (TSA) Nationwide Listing 1990–1991 through 2017–2018," *US Department of Education Office of Postsecondary Education*, May 2017, https://www2.ed.gov. Cf. Elizabeth Ross, "Databurst: Teacher Shortages and Surpluses," *National Council on Teacher Quality*, February 2018, https://www.nctq.org.
7. Grace Lin, "States that Spend the Most and Least on Education," *Yahoo Finance*, March 7, 2019, https://finance.yahoo.com.
8. Daarel Burnette II, "U.S. Spends $23 Billion More on White Districts than Nonwhite Districts, Report Says," *Education Week*, February 27, 2019, https://blogs.edweek.org.
9. Bryan Lynn, "The US Has Seen Increased Demand for Teachers in Recent Years, Some Blame the Shortage on Low Wages," *Voice of America Global Citizen*, August 23, 2018, https://www.globalcitizen.org.
10. "Mentoring New Teachers: How Can Renewed Approaches to Mentoring Help New Teachers?" *Southern Regional Education Board*, January 2018, https://www.sreb.org, 8.
11. Ibid.
12. Ibid.

13. Harry K. Wong, "Induction Programs that Keep New Teachers Teaching and Improving," *National Association of Secondary School Principals (NASSP)* 88, no. 638 (March 2004): 42.
14. "Best Practices in Teacher and Administrator Induction Programs," *California County Superintendents Educational Services Association*, June 2016, http://ccsesa.org.
15. Tustin, "Are Tougher Tests?" Cf. Elizabeth A. Harris, "Tough Tests for Teachers, with Question of Bias," *New York Times*, June 17, 2015, https://www.nytimes.com.
16. Ernest J. Zarra III, *The Wrong Direction for Today's Schools: The Impact of Common Core on American Education* (Lanham, MD: Rowman & Littlefield, 2015).
17. Rachel Tustin, "Are Tougher Tests?"
18. Ibid.
19. "Mentoring New Teachers," 1.
20. Ibid., 4–5.
21. Ibid., 5.
22. Ibid., 2–4.
23. Liam Goldrick, "Support from the Start: A 50-State Review of Policies on New Educator Induction and Mentoring," *New Teacher Center*, March 2016, https://newteachercenter.org, 13–16.
24. Julie Rowland Woods, "Mitigating Teacher Shortages: Alternative Teaching Certification," *Education Commission of the States*, May 2016, https://www.ecs.org, 4–5.
25. Mary Ellen Flannery, "Lean on Me: How Mentors Help First-Year Teachers," *NEA Today*, June 19, 2017, http://neatoday.org.
26. Ibid.
27. Ibid.
28. Kevin Richert, "Non-traditional Hires Surge amid Idaho's Teacher Shortage," *Idaho News*, September 28, 2017, https://www.idahoednews.org.
29. Ibid.
30. Sally Ho, "Public School Strikes Revive Clash with Teach for America," *Education Week*, February 14, 2019, https://www.edweek.org.
31. Teach for America, https://www.teachforamerica.org.
32. Teach for All, https://teachforall.org.
33. Ho, "Public School Strikes."
34. Ibid.
35. Richert, "Non-traditional Hires."
36. Alexis Huicochea and Yoohyun Jung, "Shortage Puts Uncertified Teachers in Arizona Classrooms," August 1, 2015. *Arizona Daily Star*, https://tucson.com.
37. Ricardo Cano, "Arizona Schools Hired 1,035 Underqualified School Teachers This School Year," *Republic*, December 13, 2017, https://www.azcentral.com.
38. Ibid.
39. Nicole Crites, "Exodus of Teachers from Arizona Classrooms," *AZFamily*, April 19, 2018, https://www.azfamily.com.
40. Cano, "Arizona Schools."
41. Ibid.
42. Jane Meredith Adams, "Most Teachers in California Say They Need More Training in Alternatives to Suspensions, Survey Finds," *EdSource*, May 7, 2017, https://edsource.org.
43. Aliyya Swaby, "Twice a Week, These Texas Students Circle Up and Talk about Their Feelings. It's Lowering Suspensions and Preventing Violence," *Texas Tribune*, May 28, 2018, https://www.texastribune.org. Cf. Emily Richmond, "When Restorative Justice in Schools Works," *Atlantic*, December 29, 2015, https://www.theatlantic.com.
44. Center for Justice and Reconciliation, http://restorativejustice.org. Cf. "What Is Restorative Justice?" *Restorative Practices International*, accessed May 9, 2019, https://rpiassn.org.
45. Sascha Brodsky, "Is Discipline Reform Really Helping Decrease School Violence?" *Atlantic*, June 28, 2016, https://www.theatlantic.com. Cf. Ernest J. Zarra III, *Assaulted: Violence in Schools and What Needs to Be Done* (Lanham, MD: Rowman & Littlefield, 2017).
46. Stephanie Aragon, "Mitigating Teacher Shortages: Financial Incentives," *Education Commission of the States*, April 27, 2016, https://www.ecs.org.

47. Woods, "Mitigating Teacher Shortages," 5.
48. Ibid.
49. Ibid.
50. Ibid.
51. "Creating a Teacher Mentoring Program," *National Foundation for the Improvement of Education (NEA)* 1 (Fall 1999): 1–2, https://www.neafoundation.org.
52. "4 Unusual Perks for Teachers That Districts Are Trying Out," *Education Week*, March 1, 2019, https://www.edweek.org.
53. Ibid.
54. Ibid.
55. Ibid.
56. "Creating a Teacher Mentoring Program."
57. Wong, "Induction Programs," 55.
58. "Guidelines for Mentor Teacher Programs for Beginning and Experienced Teachers," *Virginia State Department of Education: Division of Teacher Education and Licensure*, June 22, 2000, http://www.doe.virginia.gov.
59. "Creating a Teacher Mentoring Program."
60. Annie Holmquist, "College Illiteracy Is Growing," *Intellectual Takeout*, February 17, 2017, https://www.intellectualtakeout.org.
61. Anne Podolsky, Tara Kini, Joseph Bishop, et al., "Solving the Teacher Shortage: How to Attract and Retain Excellent Educators," *Learning Policy Institute*, September 15, 2016, https://learningpolicyinstitute.org.
62. Madeline Farber, "College Admissions Cheating Scheme: 3 Bizarre Details from the Complaint," *FoxNews*, March 12, 2019, https://www.foxnews.com.
63. Zarra, *Wrong Direction for Today's Schools*.
64. "Power and Authority," *Acton Institute*, May 9, 2019, https://acton.org.

Chapter Four

Teaching—Perception versus Reality

> This year will go down in history as a milestone year for the teaching profession. In six states, tens of thousands of teachers walked out of their classrooms to protest low salaries and cuts to school funding. Nearly 180 current classroom teachers ran for their state legislatures on a platform centered around funding education, and 43 of those teachers were elected. Suddenly, the whole country seems to be talking about how underpaid and overworked teachers are. No wonder some deemed 2018 as the year of the teacher.[1]

New teachers should know what they are getting into by choosing teaching as a career. It comes as a surprise to people to find, although educators refer to teaching as a profession, it really falls short of the definition and characteristics of being considered a profession. Education is a profession. Teaching should be considered more like a trade that involves professional tasks. So, why is this such a well-kept secret?

If teaching were ever subject to a "white coat" test of professionalism, the chances of passing this test would be quite slim. Basic understanding of the traits that usually bear the title of professional is minimal. Certainly, although used loosely, the term *professional* does not portray that of a public school teacher image. There is no amount of mentoring that will change this reality and align what amounts to a shifty perception that public school classrooms are the places where professionals hang out.

PROFESSIONALS

When people think of a professional in any field, there is a different set of characteristics than one would apply to K–12 teachers. For example, professional athletes are at the highest levels they can attain in their sport. Many of them attended college, were drafted out of high school, or spent years training in professional sports at lower levels. There is a certain skill set that is highly desired.

Whether a person thinks of physicians, lab workers, or scientists, certain attire for men and women is standard. Many professionals wear business attire or uniforms. Professionals schedule appointments with people and see clients and patients, or colleagues. As a norm, those considered as professionals do not see people in groups of twenty-five to forty, several times a day, every workday.

Teachers do not see clients, take appointments, put official signs on their doors, hang out shingles, or even cancel classes due to emergencies. Few professionals leave scripted plans, detailing all moments of the day for those that substitute for them. Someone just covers for them, or not.

Teachers cannot bill students and families for after-hours extra time working on their behalves. There are no tangible business write-offs, and even restroom time is at a premium. Physicians do not have mandatory recesses, parking lots, or bus duties for their patients. Lawyers do not take thirty-minute lunches in the lawyers' lounges, alongside the office custodians and parent volunteers. All of this has been written to close the gap between perception and reality.

Understanding this really should relax new teachers so that they can perform their duties without having to live up to work standards that are unrealistic. Far too often, the perception is not in alignment with the realities, or the demands of the job. What is taught to teachers-in-training in classes is often not the same reality they face when they are hired. Teachers are true craftsmen and craftswomen—and even perform some professional duties—but today's public school system allows for less creativity and more regimented program following. The bottom line is that teachers might be referred to as professionals, but teaching in today's public education system is certainly not a profession.

Compensation Is Not Competitive

If teaching was a true profession, then teachers could have personal agents, or even be able to negotiate their own contracts, much like people can do as experts as professionals, at the professor level at college, as athletes in professional sports, or as physicians in medicine. Expertise and professionalism are still valued in true professions. The moment a public school teacher tries to negotiate or suggest a better way for the schools, the responses would be *we could hire two people on your salary alone* and *we have to do it this way*.

Even in times of great demand, emergency substitutes are cheaper than teachers with veteran experience and tenure. The bottom line for districts and administrators is finances. What leverage do teachers have to negotiate from their vantage point, arguing that their skills as teachers make them more valuable for a public school?

Regression is not a mark of professionalism, by any stretch of the imagination. Far be it for me to disparage and diminish nearly four decades as a classroom teacher, working at all levels. There have been some wonderful experiences with stellar people who molded many lives and careers. Rather, the intent is to provide a lens of reality, so clear and real that new teachers will know exactly what they are getting into. In this way, rather than leave the classroom jaded and disappointed, reality provides greater chances for teachers to stick around. Conversely, if teachers did decide to leave, they would be leaving before the process moved too far down the road toward shell shock.

Imagine for a moment that teachers are being paid cash incentives to raise test scores, just as some baseball managers are paid for winning one hundred games, or as an athlete who earns bonuses after meeting goals of his or her contract. Such practices are not allowed in public education. In order to be fair and rule out making others feel bad, competition is disallowed and therefore there is no merit pay for teachers. The reality is that bonuses for a job well done are quite common in true professions.

However, the news is not all bad. There are incentives for teachers to sign on for "combat, or risk-taking" payments in troubled school districts in some cities. But in this case, the desperation for one warm body is worth more than another warm body, solely on the grounds of accepting the risks involved to life and limb.

Teachers can certainly become experts in many things, including teaching a content area, construction of projects, and even by a professional credential. Likewise, professional roles can be assumed and some teachers become mentors and master teachers, adding a title and maybe even a stipend. But expertise of a person in something does not elevate everyone in that group to the level of professional. Besides, when the system self-identifies and demonstrates unprofessional traits, there is only one conclusion to be drawn. Such is the case with public education.

The system asks for professionals to be placed within it, yet disallows most of the actions of true professionals. On a microscale this is equivalent to asking students to work at the highest levels, only to do so under conditions of poor curriculum, no access to technology, and with untrained teachers in broken-down buildings. The mantra of all students are excellent students does not change the system in which they learn.

The average teacher is paid to make widgets over the course of a school year, and the same is true of the next teacher. As students move on, the widgets are supposed to become better widgets. At the end of each year, whoever makes the best widgets might be celebrated by being named as *widget-maker of the year* and receive a bronze widget.

EDUCATION AS THE PROFESSION

Teachers do not officially assess students' disabilities, or learning issues. Teachers merely respond to the expert school psychologists, parent liaisons, or trained counselors. Teachers can suggest an evaluation, or possibly refer a student. In this sense, it is quite clear that professional tasks such as these actually extend far beyond the requirements of teaching.

Teachers are the gatekeepers for others with the titles that go with their professions. Even the lesson plans written by teachers have a model and template provided for them. They have very little input into the curriculum choices yet are to become well acquainted with the standards someone has developed for them to follow and target each day.

Teachers are participants in things considered professional but without the title. The reason is because teachers are generalists, especially in the elementary classrooms. This is sort of like being the Jack-of-all-trades but the master of none. The reality here is that being a good—or even great teacher—does not come with the title of *professional*. For example, all teachers know that once the school psychologist enters the classroom of even a great teacher, deference occurs.

Sarah Morrison understands that teaching is more like a trade, or a developing craft, than a profession. She writes, "Teaching is more than just standing in a room sharing what you know to a group of kids. It involves careful planning, taking the time to hone your craft and discovering how to present your information in ways that hold a child's attention."[2] However, Morrison quit the classroom for a variety of reasons addressed later in this chapter, and she is not alone.[3] Like Morrison, all teachers just want to teach.

Teacher Planning and Creativity

Since most of today's education is scripted and driven by standards and adopted curriculum, what is left to plan? Usually planning amounts to a pacing calendar, and coming to an agreement as to when one lesson or another is taught. There is very little left to decide, in terms of the "what" should be taught. These decisions are made in groups, or by administrators.

In several of the previous decades, teachers were issued a book and a teacher's edition, and possibly some materials from previous years. The onus was on them to put together what their specific class needed—including those students who today would bear labels placed on them, and accommodations designed by special services and psychologists. Disaggregating student groups has led to bringing more professionals into classrooms than there were in the past.

In an increasing number of schools in the United States, students work on curriculum on smart devices to demonstrate proficiency, and the data is printed out for the teacher. The teacher facilitates the students' interaction with their techno-curriculum. As Morrison explains, "These elements do very little to hone a teacher's craft, and even less discovering how to hold a child's attention. In reality, the device and headphones already seem to have today's students captivated."[4] Teachers now defer more often to the technology professionals, who have snagged much of the creativity from the minds of the classroom teachers.

Predictions for the Future

Predictions in the early to middle first decade of the twenty-first century called for vast improvements, higher numbers of students enrolling in teacher education programs, and an increase in teachers into the workplace. To this point, the National Center for Education Statistics (NCES) projected the number of new teacher hires in the United States to increase to nearly 30 percent between the years 2011 and 2022.[5]

The NCES also projected that teacher-student ratios would decrease during that time, as well. The facts are that the number of students projected by the year 2030 is expected to exceed fifty-five million, while the real number of teachers continues to plummet in the present. Among the many reasons given for the optimistic projections by the NCES is the rationale that students left teaching during the Great Recession of 2009, as many teachers either were let go or decided to go into other careers.[6] Also projected was that people would jump at the chance to teach once the economy rebounded. Just the opposite has occurred.

Statistical gymnastics are sometimes employed to justify projections in education. For example, much has been made about a few states that have reported surpluses of teachers. In Massachusetts, for example, this was the reasoning used for some to conclude that there is not a national teacher shortage but merely disproportionate placements of people with teaching credentials. The theory spread that if the nation could somehow reallocate these teachers, there would be less of a perceived shortage.

The reality is, in rural areas of many states, numbers of applicants for teachers are down. As mentioned earlier in this book, one of the driving factors for decreases in applicants is low teacher pay for the work required. However, even in states where the starting pay is higher, such as in California, some "80% of districts reported a shortage of qualified teachers in 2017–2018, and nine out of 10 of those districts said the situation was worse than the previous school year. California has about 305,000 total teachers in K–12 public schools."[7] So, the perception that higher pay brings more teachers does not square with reality. Something has changed in our culture, and people are choosing to work in jobs outside of teaching. This had led to extreme measures being taken by some states.

Extreme Measures

Some states are resorting to extreme measures in order to stem the tide of teacher attrition. For example, in the state of Washington, out of desperation, when there is "no other option, school districts can hire people without teaching certificates—or even a college degree—to fill temporary teacher vacancies. . . . The districts with highest percentages of emergency teachers tend to be small, with many students from low-income families."[8] This practice is becoming more widespread. The saddest part of all of this, as Emily Eng suggests, is that "kids in poverty need to have the most credentialed, effective teachers if they're going to get out of poverty."[9]

The desperate measures of Washington State are not necessarily the same as in Colorado. In the fall of 2018, the Denver public schools piloted a program "aimed at training new teachers in the buildings where they are most likely to be assigned: the city's high-poverty schools."[10] However, at the same time, the city of Denver became so expensive to live in that teachers resorted to creative measures, such as securing second and third jobs, in order to meet their monthly financial requirements.[11]

According to the Learning Policy Institute, "turnover rates are 50 percent higher in under-resourced schools," and each teacher that quits from an urban school district can wind up costing that school district nearly $20,000.[12] A recent study of sixteen urban school districts that served approximately 2.5 million students annually yielded the following reasons that teachers leave in the first place. The following five findings coincide with the fact that just over half of the new teachers remained in the classrooms after five years on the job. These findings illustrate "important trends about teacher retention."[13]

- The percentage of teachers who left their jobs within five years was about 75 percent.
- Although staying in the same districts, only one in five teachers remained at the same schools for five years.
- About half the teachers in districts returned after going on some sort of leave.
- Some urban teachers leave their districts for other districts.
- Effective teachers have higher retention rates.

The bottom line in the study is that a Band-Aid approach to solving immediate shortages cannot solve the shortage problem at its root. This is illustrated by the research that "revealed no obvious, simple way to improve teacher retention."[14] However, the research is also clear that a good first step is "working to build more supportive school environments."[15]

Real Teachers, Real Talk

The following excerpts are parts of comments sent by teachers from across the United States, in answer to a social media survey prompt that was posted on a national teacher's website. In each statement listed below, the reader can assume multiple similar responses were posted. After tallying the responses, each was placed into a representative category that captured the essence of the respondents' statements.

The names and locations of the respondents have been purposely left out to secure their anonymity. The prompt to which teachers were asked their opinion is "Please share your reasons for the migration of teachers away from careers in the classrooms."

- Administrative demands and parent expectations.
- Micromanagement from the state and local administrations who have little experience in the classrooms. For example, if we stray from our schedule of minutes, we are docked on our school-wide audits.
- Student discipline not being handled in a way that allows teachers to do our jobs.
- Overemphasis on test scores and teaching to the test. Data-driven dominance in every aspect of teaching and the diminishing of the human teacher/student relationship.
- Higher health-care costs. Reduced salary.
- Lack of respect from community and parents.
- Very long hours. No time for training.
- Increase in student behavior issues without support in the classroom.
- Low pay. Lousy benefits. No respect. No control over what we teach.
- Poor behavior goes unchecked.
- Increased workload.
- Stress on personal lives and families.
- Inability to afford housing.
- The push from the top down is killing my love for teaching. Eighteen years in, and I am trying to figure out something else to do.
- This is my seventeenth year, and I don't know if I can keep going. I have two kids in lower grades, and I feel horrible they are going to have teachers who feel this way.
- This is my nineteenth year, and I feel like a manager and not a teacher.
- Disrespect from student and parents and a lack of support from administration.
- Students are encouraged in their entitlement mentality. Parents all think their kids deserve an A, even with all their late work.
- Students cannot be forced to do anything, including to take responsibility.

- It's a tiring, never-ending, underappreciated job that is never close to being done. The stress isn't worth it.
- I feel so ill equipped for today's child! I am a great teacher but not a counselor or special education teacher.
- Paradox: Differentiation but not creativity.
- No spark of intellectual curiosity.
- Technological device addiction.
- Tired of the politics at all levels.
- Our state pays us so little we have to have second jobs if we still want to remain in the classroom.
- Every parent thinks their child deserves full attention like they are the only ones we teach.
- I am not a special education teacher!

This list, or at least one like it, should be distributed to all newer teachers as to what many teachers across the United States feel like at the beginning of their school years as teachers. The survey in question was taken in October 2018.

Training teachers for a world that does not exist only complicates and confuses. If their world is colored with only optimism, success, and smiles, they are receiving only one-half of the real story. So where does all of this leave America's students?

DESERVING STUDENTS

"Every student deserves a great teacher."[16] That is a nice ideal and a great meme for a bumper sticker. It probably even gets votes, but it can never be realized beyond the rhetoric. New teachers need to comprehend that statements such as these are outplayed by reality all day, every day. Maybe those who come up with these slogans should join in the education process to apply their slogans in a more tangible way. The understanding of the depths of teaching means to go far beyond the oneness of a slogan of identity.

Certainly such phrases are tailor-made for Gen Z, which considers entitlement as a right in their lives. Gen Z teachers are now out and about, and some of them are even working as newer classroom teachers. The next decade will be quite telling as they teach those from within their own generation. Determining what it means to be great for others should at least be applicable to the ones making these determinations.

It might as well be said that every teacher deserves great students and great families. These great students and great families deserve a teacher trained at the highest levels, with graduate degrees, and come into their careers with veteran-like skills and an in-depth understanding of the students and culture within which they work. But what is deserved and what is real illustrate the difference between idealism and realism.

Great students and great parents do not deserve emergency credentialed teachers, those from pathways that shortcut, or lack the requisite, training from day one.[17] A teacher's greatness depends a lot on the very students and families with whom he or she works. Greatness is made over time, and the fact is teachers are not sticking around long enough to become great.

Inasmuch as accomplished professional athletes are not guaranteed to translate their accomplishments into professional coaching, greatness in one profession may not translate to excellence in another. In today's age of teacher shortages, students deserve to have teachers that choose to stay more than one full year. Yet, in real terms, how does this square with teacher greatness?

Reality Speaks

A standard measure of how *great* teachers are is often judged in how much of themselves they give away to their students. Whether it is their time, emotions, activities, leadership, program involvement, extra duties, or even personal wellness, teacher greatness is difficult to measure. Certainly, teacher greatness is often not mentioned in the same breath as rising test scores, or diligence in the grading of papers. Ironically, a teacher can be horrible at instruction yet be viewed as one of the greatest teachers at the same time. This depends on two things: (1) what the measure is and (2) who established the measure.

The reality is that "new teachers are often faced with overwhelming workloads. They are frequently assigned the most challenging students, asked to teach multiple subjects, required to teach classes for which they are not certified, and assigned responsibility for overseeing extracurricular activities."[18] The facts are that annually somewhere between 2,000 and 2,200 providers of teacher preparation go about their tasks—whether online, in-seat, or by some hybrid or alternative pathway.

The numbers of trained teachers reach up to the hundreds of thousands by these programs.[19] Yet the sobering reality is that in 2015, Teach Plus conducted a poll of 1,020 teachers and found "77 percent said they were either not fully prepared or not at all prepared to be effective teachers."[20]

Teacher training institutions should really drill down into their programs and query themselves. They might benefit from a retooling of their mission and examining why they are using their model for training. They should also ask what areas teachers need to focus on in order to be most effective with today's Gen Z students. They could do this much better if they stopped asking administrators and superintendents what teachers need and made concerted efforts to query the very classrooms teachers they had trained and placed into public schools.

One of the more interesting facts about institutions that train teachers is that up until recently, "knowledge and information about how well graduates of teacher training programs performed was generally limited to the institutions that trained them. Teacher education programs could collect data on their graduates through surveys or other feedback tools to hear how their training prepared them for their work in schools."[21]

Successes and failures could be kept largely in-house. But times are changing, and states are coming at the current problems from different vantage points, some of which are prompted by desperate legislators.

STATES GETTING SERIOUS

Lately, states have undertaken efforts to research and develop what legislators believe are "systemic solutions to improving teacher preparation . . . utilizing state-level departments of education . . . and report data about teacher education programs in their state. While these reports vary from state to state, they can include characteristics and information about teachers in training as well as how graduates of the program fare once they are in schools."[22]

States are beginning to share information. This is where new teachers would be able to make a difference with their feedback about their first years of experience. But are they even queried, is the question?

In calendar year 2012, the Council of Chief State School Officers (CCSSO) Taskforce on Educator Preparation and Entry into the Profession released the report titled "Our Responsibility, Our Promise." The report was written "as a call to action to state chiefs to use their authority over three policy levers to ensure every teacher is learner-ready and every principal is school-ready on Day 1."[23]

To the seasoned veteran, this call to action smacks of the mandate set forth under No Child Left Behind. Under NCLB, the nation was focused on the goal of getting every group and every subgroup moved from far below basic to basic and then on to proficient. The stated goal by 2014 was 100 percent proficiency. The goal of all teachers being learner-ready on their first day of teaching is just as absurd as the mandate was under NCLB.

After CCSSO (2013) launched the NTEP (Network for Transforming Educator Preparation), seven states aligned to form a network. This network's purpose was to collaborate and examine areas of their teacher education programs that were in need of being revamped and changed. After several additional years of study, and data contributions to the CCSSO, by state Teacher Preparation Analytics (TPAs; 2016), the CCSSO had collected data from thirty states (2018).[24]

The CCSSO released its results in 2018 and—along with major policy recommendations for teacher education programs—the document had an impact on teacher education in the United States. The following policy recommendations were based on findings of the study.[25]

- Teachers believe the quality of a preparation program is best measured by the performance of its graduates as classroom teachers and believe that the diversity of its candidates and their retention in schools and districts are important factors in the attractiveness of the program.
- Teachers overwhelmingly support the idea that states should hold teacher preparation programs accountable for how well they train their educators.
- Teachers want states to regularly release reports on teacher preparation programs that are transparent and accessible.
- Teachers believe aspiring educators should pay attention to the indicators of classroom performance of program graduates, but also to how well teacher preparation programs provide them with a strong knowledge base on which to grow professionals.

Teach Plus is another organization that collected survey data. The group used a mixed-method research approach in its collection as it convened focus groups and surveyed teachers in public schools. The results of the survey aligned with several results of the CCSSO,[26] including the following:

- The teachers surveyed believe that producing graduates who know what and how to teach both generally and within their specific content areas is critical.
- It became evident in the voices of teachers that having a diverse faculty was important for many reasons, particularly for preparing teachers who would reflect the populations of students they serve.
- Teachers also had strong feelings about teacher retention and turnover and reflected that when discussing reports showing how many candidates remained in the profession after being in the classroom for a short time and how that was important to determining the success of a program.

STATES REDUCING REQUIREMENTS

Teach Plus's findings "suggest that aspiring educators take into consideration a wide variety of factors when deciding to embark on the journey to become a teacher. Personal factors such as proximity to family and friends, as well as other factors such as flexibility and graduation rate all play an important role in deciding which program the prospective teacher chose to attend."[27] Now that states are serious they have begun to employ creative measures.

States are finding creative ways to recruit teachers. North Carolina has decided to scrap their Pearson state math licensing exam in favor of a Praxis math test developed by the nonprofit organization ETS. Thousands of North Carolina teachers have failed the examination more than once. "Teachers are complaining because the $139 tests get expensive when they have to repeatedly retake them, while others allege it could ultimately cost them a career they're otherwise well suited for."[28]

Members of the North Carolina Professional Educator Preparation and Standards Commission pointed out that the math licensing examination is "not an indicator of an effective teacher."[29] In addition, many claim that the exam "is a barrier to licensure and that trickles down to . . . vacancies in the class and a teacher shortage."[30]

States using Pearson math exams for licensure are finding similar trends. "States including Florida and Indiana"[31] are having to revise their teacher education requirements, after seeing drops in mathematics scores. Meanwhile, Pearson responded that states set their own rates of passage on assessments and that it "does not place any artificial barriers in the way of candidate success and only considers test scores as criteria for passage."[32]

Apparently, the passing scores set by states are not being met by teachers. The easiest thing to do is to blame the assessment for being too difficult and drop the assessment for a less rigorous exam. This leaves state officials in some states scratching their heads and thinking, "Instead of considering ways colleges can better educate future teachers to pass the tests, the focus thus far has remained mostly on whether the Pearson test is too rigorous."[33] Could another issue be the supply of candidates?

STATES GETTING A HANDLE ON RETAINING TEACHERS

There are a number of points of emphasis that bear noting. Each of these points, when taken separately, alone might not affect teacher attrition. Yet when taken together, understanding the chances and likelihood of retaining teachers improves. Getting a handle on teacher retention is best approached from a corporate mindset. This mindset includes a nine-factor conceptual framework that builds an approach, focusing squarely on teacher retention.[34]

These nine factors are as follows:

1. Involving the principals in any discussions regarding teacher shortages. The principals are on the ground and understand the dynamics of the schools in question.
2. Drawing in the district administration for brainstorming sessions and asking what they are doing to deal with the problems of teacher shortages in their schools.

3. Reading and reviewing what the US Department of Education, the Learning Policy Institute, and other professional organizations suggest to reduce attrition and retain teachers.
4. Grouping that takes the ideas to the state level and presents them to state legislatures for consideration. The presenters must focus not only on the problems but also on suggested solutions gathered from the research and data provided by organizations.
5. Teaming up with colleges and teacher education institutions to revise programs and offer incentives to attract and retain teachers to careers of working with children.
6. Experimenting with delivery models for teachers-in-training. For example, teacher residencies are often good strategies and should be implemented.
7. Developing a structure that widens the loan/debt forgiveness in mind for teachers willing to commit to becoming tenured.
8. Offering practical and timely professional development to continue to equip teachers with the information and practicum necessary for ongoing success with today's student.
9. Mentoring each teacher and allowing them plenty of classroom practice, fully supported by an induction program that focuses on success and retention.

CONCERNS FOR WELLNESS

An issue discussed more increasingly in teacher education institutions, and within the pages education literature, is teacher wellness. The difference between perception and reality can be life altering. The past few years have seen disturbingly real rises in the increase of the numbers of college students who are in need of mental health treatment and care.

One might not consider this an issue within a discussion of teacher preparation. Drawing this conclusion could not be farther from the truth. Going forward, in terms of recruiting applicants to teacher education programs, faculty must be concerned about the stressors that accompany any eventual rigor associated with teacher training.

A 2017 study conducted by the American Psychiatric Association of 155,000 college students, from 196 institutions, revealed that the "rate of respondents being treated for mental health issues . . . increased to 34 percent in 2017 from 19 percent in 2007, while the percentage of students with lifetime diagnoses increased to 3 percent from 22 percent. Depression and suicide risks also increased. . . . But the stigma of being diagnosed with a mental illness decreased, which could explain some of the increases."[35]

Findings like these lead to wellness concerns for students as they move forward into their careers, notwithstanding and including education and teaching. If there are serious needs that manifest themselves while students are training to be teachers, what is the measure used to determine there is not high risk upon entrance into the day-to-day risk environment of the classroom? It is at this juncture that there are clear crossovers from perceptions to reality.

According to John Davies, Roxanne Davis, and Sue Heacock, "On-site wellness programs have the potential to attract qualified employees and to positively affect productivity and efficiency . . . besides the health benefits, wellness programs can have a positive effect on teamwork, morale, and teacher effectiveness."[36] This is very important for all teachers, and time should be carved out for them while they are still in training.

A research study published in the 2018 issue of the *Journal of American College Health* confirmed the increase of mental illness among today's undergraduates. Lead researcher Sara Oswalt of the University of Texas, San Antonio, writes, "Between 2009 and 2015, treatment and diagnoses of anxiety increased nearly 6 percent . . . followed by depression and panic attacks. . . . Anxiety is the most common problem, affecting almost 15 percent of college students across the United States."[37] How will anxiety play out in the lives of newer teachers who seem to have more diagnoses of anxiety disorders than veteran teachers?[38]

Oswalt added that among the 450,000 college undergraduates surveyed, "it's not clear if the college environment is causing or even contributing to the increase in these problems. But . . . more students are seeking help because more of them are suffering from mental health problems, coupled with a willingness to get help. There is less stigma about mental health issues, and schools may be providing more mental health services. . . . Because 75% of all serious adult psychiatric illnesses start by age 25, universities have an essential role in addressing mental health issues early."[39]

Just at the time that college students' brains wire up in their early to midtwenties, mental illness is somehow being discovered. Time can only tell what these revelations may lead to in practical terms for eventual public school teachers.

General Implications for College Students

What are some of the implications of college students seeking mental health therapy and treatments? First, does the increase of students with mental health issues provide evidence that not all students are meant for the rigors of college, at least at the ages they are attending?

Second, what is the extent that students coming to college and universities are already saddled with serious issues, which may be chronicled by 504 accommodations, or earlier individualized education program (IEP) placement from elementary school through high school? Third, if the rigors of college are unhealthy places for those with mental illnesses, and placing them with children is not wise, then which majors are best suited for those with conditions such as anxiety and depression who may be prone to missing work?

General Implications for Future Teachers

Generally, what percentage of those with serious mental illness find themselves in teacher education programs, training to work in a high-stress environment? Conversely, how many students would shy away from teaching, given that their conditions might not allow their efforts to be most effective? Either way, wellness is in question.

Teacher recruit numbers might be terribly affected by more stringent acceptance requirements. However, with all likelihood, because of a teacher shortage that would probably never become a serious issue to legislators. Attention must be drawn to the reality that the placement of high-risk students in high-risk environments is too great a risk all around.

What percentage of teachers with persistent mental health issues is acceptable in public schools? Furthermore, what percentage of teachers are involved in the increase of inappropriate emotional and/or sexual relationships with students? It is best to have some semblance of answers to these questions before teachers are offered contracts to work with students.

At issue then is when should these concerns be addressed? Should they become part of teacher induction programs? Are they best addressed throughout mentoring, or by means of periodic and thematic professional development? Legislators and school administrators have to make up their minds as to how serious they really are about these issues. The mental health of teachers does have implications upon the proper development of relationships with colleagues, students, and parents. Likewise, the lasting effects of improper relationships last far beyond the classroom in any given academic year.

Thousands of teachers have been dismissed from their jobs for everything from inappropriate actions or words toward students to being arrested for sending nude photos and meeting regularly for sex. Criminal actions of teachers who are sexually active with multiple adult partners and children risk infecting students. This is another aspect of wellness and not only for the teacher.

In addition to the reality of these concerns, there are also false allegations of sexual misconduct that enter into the mix. These can lead to a dismissal of employment, or reassignment, simply because of bad press. Families of teachers that endure these false allegations are often forced to move from the area. Teachers shy away from the classrooms because of fear of such damage to their careers. New teachers are especially easy targets. So, what is the impact on education? One of the impacts is that some people will not choose teaching as a career because of this fear,[40] and it is not just a fear for teachers in the United States.[41]

TEACHERS AND AUTHENTICITY

Authentic instruction emerges from teachers who approach their content from a perspective that has removed as much "personal" bias as possible. Although bias is an eventual and seemingly inescapable reality in society, teachers have to be on guard to counter its encroachment upon the classroom. This can be done by recognizing a few things early on. Jinnie Spiegler argues for authenticity in early grades and at earlier ages in schools:

> As a society and within our educational institutions, discussions about bias, diversity, discrimination, and social justice tend to happen in middle and high schools. We've somehow decided that little kids can't understand these complex topics, or we want to delay exposing them to injustices as long as possible (even though not all children have the luxury of being shielded from injustice). Racial identity and attitudes begin to develop in children at a young age. Two- and three-year-olds become aware of the differences between boys and girls, may begin noticing obvious physical disabilities, become curious about skin color and hair color/texture, and may also be aware of ethnic identity.... In terms of bias, by age three or four, white children in the U.S., Canada, Australia, and Europe show preferences for other white children. Further current research suggests that children as young as three years old, when exposed to prejudice and racism, tend to embrace and accept it even though they may not understand the feelings. The good news is that bias can be unlearned or reversed if we're exposed to diversity in a positive way.... Elementary school is a time ripe for these discussions.... Here are five concrete ways of bringing discussions about bias and diversity into the classroom: (1) Use children's literature. (2) Use the news media. (3) Teach anti-bias lessons. (4) Give familiar examples. (5) Explore solutions.... We need to begin this process with our youngest hearts and minds in order to have a lasting impact.[42]

Authentic content begins by verification from a variety of primary and secondary sources, some of which may be authentic to the period in which instruction is anchored. Authentic instruction is not content alone. Authenticity sprinkled into the lives of students brings yet another level of authenticity: *authentic learning*. Authentic learning has a correlation and application to other contexts. The more relevant to a student's life, the more authentic the instruction. Likewise, the more authentic the instruction, the more authentic the teacher is to the learner. It is here, then, that a teacher can make every effort to thwart the majority of bias from affecting the classroom in a major way as he or she makes major connections.

Making Emotional Connections

Students that are emotionally engaged in content experience both cognitive challenge and satisfaction through interesting and purposeful learning. When taken together, these two comprise a large part of effective engagement on the parts of learners. Students, after all, learn best when their brains are engaged and their cranial pleasure chemicals swim freely, if you will.

Authentic teachers can use personal stories to grab hold of the learners. In this way, learning becomes real for the students. They can teach as if they are acting in a Hollywood movie. However, authenticity at all levels requires not just an authentic teacher story but also content delivered through varied stories and personalized cognitive and emotional connections. Such is the task of the authentic classroom conduit, called the teacher.

Learning is decisive and incisive. When teachers love what they teach, and love whom it is they teach, the cylinders of learning are fueled by the incendiary of instruction. There is no better place for teachers to begin their careers than with a basic understanding of human authenticity. The old common adage still rings true: *the students do not care what you know, if they do not know that you care.*

GETTING REAL ABOUT OFFSETTING TEACHER SHORTAGES

According to Kate Walsh, the president of the National Council on Teacher Quality, "Some school systems with severe shortages have changed certification requirements to bring in more teachers. Others have decided to permit the hiring of teachers with little, or in some case, no classroom experience. In some states . . . officials are lowering some quality requirements too much in an attempt to find enough teachers. There have been a number of states which have made some decisions that we think run counter to teacher quality goals."[43]

Dan Goldhaber, the director for the Center for Education Data and Research at the University of Washington, maintains that some reasons for the teacher shortage are due to the unwillingness of some states to recognize the licensure and credentialing of other states. He states the "teacher labor markets are pretty localized and each state has different licensure systems, so it's not like you can easily hire someone to teach in California who is a teacher in Massachusetts. We do not have that kind of a national teacher labor market."[44]

In terms of alternative programs offered by states, the "Alternative Teacher Certification Guide"[45] is a comprehensive document providing helpful links to all states and many alternative programs for people seeking to become teachers. An example of this document is provided in appendix B, where a sample of eight select states and their provisions for certification acquisition via alternative pathways is provided.

Helpful Programs?

The Paul Douglas Teacher Scholarship Program, which was formerly the Congressional Teacher Scholarship Program, offers scholarships to students who are "generally required to teach for two years for every year of scholarship assistance received."[46] The caveat for the scholarship was that it was less constraining for schools where the federal government officially identified and designated a higher need for teachers. If a teacher applied to any of these schools, he or she was required "to teach only one year for each year of scholarship assistance received."[47]

The Teacher Education Assistance for College and Higher Education (TEACH) grant program

> provides grants of up to $4000 per year to students who agree to serve as a highly qualified full-time teacher in a high-need field in a public of private elementary or secondary school that serves students from low-income families. A TEACH grant recipient must teach for at least four academic years within eight years of completing the program of study for which the TEACH Grant was received. If the . . . recipient fails to complete the service requirement, the total amount of . . . funds received will be converted to a . . . Federal Direct Unsubsidized Loan.[48]

As an attempt at another financial incentive to reverse the decline in teacher candidate enrollments, the state of California is lobbying for the return of federal grants for student loan forgiveness as incentives for college students to again consider teaching as a career. These federal grants "helped to support students through the preparation process" during the mid-2010s.[49] California politicians want them back now.

Considering the Alternatives: Traditional versus Nontraditional

There are several key reasons that alternative models of certification may be neither the most efficient nor the most practical ways to prepare teachers for real-world classrooms. One recruit from a nontraditional model, Teach for America, writes,

> Once I was teaching, I had education classes two nights a week after working a nine-hour day, weekend professional development, and regular meetings with my supervisor. At the same time, I was expected to teach while, truth be told, I was still learning how to do it. My students were guinea pigs, and I was

exhausted. Sure, I could plan a year's worth of standards-based units over a weekend, but was I truly prepared to face the kids on Monday? I felt that I was wildly reaching in the direction of good teaching while never having time to work toward true mastery of the craft.[50]

In contrast to the TFA model, a teacher recruit from a traditional model shares,

> In my traditional program, when it came time to plan a classroom management system, I had already spent more than 100 hours observing master educators in several classrooms and had been part of a cohort of preservice teachers for almost a year. I had seen management systems in action, read about them in books and articles, written about them for my professors, and talked them over with my colleagues. In this second attempt at preparing a management system, I felt much less harried and much more knowledgeable.[51]

There are several elements that must be considered, between traditional and nontraditional teacher education models. First, there is the issue of flexibility. One must ask whether he or she has the time to sit face-to-face in classes, or even the time to make deadlines for work in traditional programs or within other program avenues. Also, there are incentives for students to take courses online because there is the perception that more time exists for course completion. This is not the case. Another incentive is the class work can be tended to according to the schedule of the student and is not locked in for a certain day, or time. Additionally, some students find better financial flexibility to afford online seminar classes without all of the extra college and possibly travel costs.[52]

It would appear that the conventional wisdom for twenty-first-century higher education is that "traditional classes are now considered more suitable for young children, teenagers, and young adolescents who are yet to join the workforce. Regular attendance in classes helps them interact with other individuals of their own age, be better disciplined, follow a regular schedule, and improve their physical fitness and mental alertness."[53] Once students hit college, both full time and part time, education should favor the student and his or her access, rather than fit a prescribed routine of classes only. However, what about the value of face-to-face instruction?

As one author states, "Traditional, in-class settings may also offer more opportunities for spur-of-the-moment questioning of interesting tangents that may help a concept 'click' in the minds of students,"[54] where students can "directly share their views and clarify their own queries . . . thus getting their questions answered right away."[55] Usually in online classes, the learner is not directly interacting with the faculty. So, when students have questions, "they may find it difficult to ask their online instructor, as communication is often very impersonal."[56] To offset this shortcoming, "often these courses offer alternatives to live query resolution like online forums, emails, and chatrooms."[57]

Furthermore, students in face-to-face classes can ask many questions, cover many concepts, and "in the long run, improve student performance and competence in the field of specialization."[58] The bottom line for students is their purpose for the learning. "A student can look at it from the perspective of flexibility, affordability, practicality and discipline of taking classes. It's upon the student to decide which education system, between online and traditional, to enroll in."[59] It all comes down to accessing the knowledge and the development of the practical skills needed for a given field or career.

WHAT ABOUT ONLINE TEACHER EDUCATION

An online education "can work better for some while for others the traditional on-campus education is the best for pursuing"[60] the outcome of a college degree. All things considered, most colleges and students have come to accept the reality that "online education is simply the perfect way to strike a balance between work, family, and studies."[61] It is not going to go away.

Traditional face-to-face teacher education is being vanquished by modern approaches to training the next generation of teachers. The teacher shortage is a driver for these newer and more student-friendly programs. Still, as with all programs that are new, there are tradeoffs, costs, and consequences. Conversely, some of the benefits of online teacher education programs come down on the side of attempting to reduce teacher shortages by consciously offering access to programs that minimize interruptions to student's daily lives. The perception is that online education is just as good as face-to-face instruction. Teacher educators do not agree with this perception.

Counterintuitive Programs

Teaching is first and foremost about people. At most levels, whom teachers teach is much more important than what teachers teach. Certainly the ages of the students, their families, and of course their teachers will vary. Online teacher education programs are most counterintuitive to the very nature of the reality that teachers will face each day.

Teachers training online will wind up shortchanged for the very jobs they hope to pursue. Online training is being criticized for the way it is presented because it is not preparing students for the real world they will face. All things considered, it might come as a surprise to discover that online classes and programs in education have their place. If the philosophy of the program is to fill the needs created by shortages, then expediency over sufficiency is the fundamental rationale for colleges to offer these programs. By all means online teacher education is then beneficial.

Students today tend to view training to become a teacher more difficult through traditional programs. Therefore colleges must provide the incentives necessary to motivate students to choose in-seat education. But changing perceptions is good. The fact is, "online education programs are well established in higher education, including graduate level and nontraditional teacher education programs."[62] Gen Z, primarily, wants education their way and with the luxury of education according to their preference of time slots. This is their reality for the twenty-first century.

Benefits and Costs

Teachers trained online and later expected to excel face-to-face in the classroom are placing extreme pressure on the teacher overseeing the online trained person. If the first time a trainee is exposed to comprehensive teaching of students is around the time of his or her student teaching, or internship, then this places immense pressure on the in-class mentor/advisor. Sometimes, because of geographical distance, there is not a professor either online or present to oversee the student teachers in action. Hopefully, access to real classrooms and teaching are all embedded as parts of online teacher education courses.

The better places for an online program that involve teachers seem to be graduate programs, where research and professorial interactions are based less on face-to-face training and more on research and writing. There is more to teaching than knowledge and comprehension. There are real relationships that are built and there are strong correlations among teacher training, teacher success in the classroom, and these relationships. The warm-body approach to education is behind much of what is evolving nationally, and it is a shame that one has to wonder about the disparity of online training and the real world of working with people, in terms of turnover rate and attrition. Some of the unintended consequences that result from such high rates of turnover are the costs to train new teachers, the relationships that never truly develop, and schools with newer teachers who are not enabled to mature into the job to see the larger context of career longevity. Test scores usually plummet with newer teachers. High rates of teacher turnover cannot be assumed to produce higher test score for students.

CONCLUSION

Researchers are quick to point out they do not expect online teacher education programs to completely replace traditional face-to-face programs any time soon. However, hybrid programs and parallel face-to-face and online program offerings, where weaknesses of one method of learning may be balanced with the strengths of the other, seem to be gaining in popularity. For example, "accounting for a student's individual attention span is . . . an issue in traditional classrooms . . . and there is no way to adjust for that in a real-time environment."[63] Online classes allow students to review and rework their ideas at a slower pace, especially after they lose focus for a time.

Another way to put it is that each online student would be treated as an individual and have the sense that he or she has his or her own class. Professors might not relish dedicating the time to each individual online, especially when numbers float upward in programs. Theoretically, there would be virtual office hours. But what happens when these hours do not match the hours of many of the students in an online class, especially with time zones in the United States? International students add another dimension for consideration. Online programs might be good for students today, but the reality for professors is that they are a lot more extra work with fewer returns for the efforts.

Realistically, unless professors were dedicated to be available when it fits all of their students' schedules, there would be serious gaps in available meeting times and students might be a bit frustrated by that. The bottom line for teacher education is best captured by Deepak Reddy, who writes, "True mobility and access to education is the future . . . [but] that doesn't mean we stop empowering our classrooms and teachers."[64] It may be too late to reenergize the masses, because reality wins over perception in the end.

NOTES

1. Madeline Will, "The Teaching Profession in 2018 (in Charts)," *EdWeek*, December 14, 2018, https://blogs.edweek.org.

2. Sarah Morrison, "Why I Quit Teaching: An Insider's Look into the Struggles of Modern Teachers," *Mermaid Traveler Blog*, Bored Teachers, October 6, 2018, https://www.boredteachers.com.

3. Ibid.

4. Ibid.

5. "Missing Elements in the Discussion of Teacher Shortages," National Center for Analysis of Longitudinal Data in Education Research (CALDER), *American Institutes for Research*, 2015, https://caldercenter.org.

6. "Career Paths of Beginning School Teachers," *National Center for Education Statistics (NCES)*, US Department of Education, 2015, https://nces.ed.gov.

7. Sarah Betancourt, "Teacher Shortages Worsening in Majority of US States, Study Reveals," *Guardian*, September 6, 2018, https://www.theguardian.com. Cf. "Your Comprehensive Guide to Teaching Certification," Teacher Certification Degrees, November 11, 2018, https://www.teachercertificationdegrees.com.

8. Emily M. Eng, "School Stats: The Number of Emergency Teachers in Washington Classrooms Has Doubled," *Seattle Times*, May 17, 2017, https://www.seattletimes.com.

9. Ibid.

10. Brenda Iasevoli, "New Teachers Are Often Assigned to High-Poverty Schools. Why Not Train Them There?" *EdWeek*, August 3, 2018, http://blogs.edweek.org.

11. Christina Zdanowicz, "Denver Is So Expensive That Teachers Have to Get Creative to Make Ends Meet," *CNN*, February 11, 2019, https://www.cnn.com.

12. Desiree Carver-Thomas and Linda Darling-Hammond, "Teacher Turnover: Why It Matters and What We Can Do about It," *Learning Policy Institute*, August 2017, https://learningpolicyinstitute.org.
13. John Papay, Andrew Bacher-Hicks, Lindsay Page, et al., "America's Teacher Shortage Can't Be Solved by Hiring More Unqualified Teachers," *Washington Post*, January 9, 2018, https://www.washingtonpost.com.
14. Ibid.
15. Ibid.
16. Kevin Cormier, Timothy Hilton, and Mark Teoh, "Teach Plus," 2018, https://teachplus.org.
17. Ibid.
18. Richard W. Riley, "Eliminating Barriers to Improving Teaching," Initiative on Teaching, *US Department of Education*, November 2000, https://files.eric.ed.gov. Cf. Heather Voke, *Keeping Good Teachers*, ed. Marge Scherer (Alexandria, VA: Association for Supervision and Curriculum Development, 2003), chaps. 1–2.
19. Cormier, Hilton, and Teoh, "Teach Plus."
20. Ibid.
21. Ibid.
22. Ibid.
23. "Our Responsibility, Our Promise: Transforming Educator Preparation and Entry into the Profession," *Council of Chief State School Officers*, 2012, https://ccsso.org.
24. "Transforming Educator Preparation: Lessons Learned from Leading States," Council of Chief State School Officers, 2017, https://www.ccsso.org.
25. Cormier, Hilton, and Teoh, "Teach Plus."
26. Ibid.
27. Ibid.
28. Victor Skinner, "North Carolina to Scrap Math License Exam—After Thousands of Teachers Fail It," *EAG News*, December 19, 2018, http://eagnews.org.
29. Ibid.
30. Ibid.
31. Ibid.
32. Ibid.
33. Ibid.
34. Linda Darling-Hammond, Joyce Elliott, Desiree Carver-Thomas, et al., "Resources: Teacher Shortages in the United States," *Learning Policy Institute*, August 17, 2018, https://learningpolicyinstitute.org.
35. Paul Fain, "More Students Are Being Treated for Mental Health Issues," *Inside Higher Ed*, November 6, 2018, https://www.insidehighered.com.
36. John Davies, Roxanne Davis, and Sue Heacock, "A Wellness Program for Faculty," *Educational Leadership* 60, no. 8 (May 2003): 68–70, http://www.ascd.org.
37. Steven Reinberg, "More College Students Seeking Mental Health Care," *Health Day*, October 25, 2018, https://consumer.healthday.com.
38. Ibid.
39. Ibid.
40. Heather Piper, "False Child Abuse Allegations Take a Heavy Toll on Teachers," *Conversation*, January 20, 2014, https://theconversation.com.
41. Caroline Winter, "Risk of False Sex Abuse Claims Turning Young Men Off Teaching Careers, Union Fears," *ABC*, May 12, 2014, https://www.abc.net.au.
42. Jinnie Spiegler, "Teaching Young Children about Bias, Diversity, and Social Justice," *Edutopia*, June 16, 2016, https://www.edutopia.org. Cf. Michael Novak, "Social Justice: Not What You Think It Is," *Heritage Foundation*, December 29, 2009, https://www.heritage.org.
43. Lynn, "US Has Seen Increased Demand."
44. Ibid.
45. "Alternative Teacher Certification Guide," 2019, https://www.teachercertificationdegrees.com.

46. Freddie Cross, "Teacher Shortage Areas (TSA) Nationwide Listing 1990–1991 through 2017–2018," *US Department of Education Office of Postsecondary Education*, May 2017, https://www2.ed.gov.

47. Ibid.

48. Ibid.

49. Pat Maio, "Number of New Math and Science Teachers Declining in California," *EdSource*, April 4, 2016, https://edsource.org.

50. Genie Albina, "Which Is Better? Alternative or Traditional?" *Educational Leadership* 69, no. 8 (May 2012): 70–72, http://www.ascd.org.

51. Ibid.

52. Echo Brown, "Online Education vs. Traditional Education: Which One Is Better?" *ezTalks*, June 1, 2017, https://www.eztalks.com.

53. Barinda De, "Traditional Learning vs. Online Learning," *eLearning Industry*, February 4, 2018.

54. Will Erstad, "Online vs. Traditional Education: What You Need to Know," *Rasmussen College*, August 16, 2017, https://www.rasmussen.edu.

55. De, "Traditional Learning."

56. Ibid.

57. Ibid.

58. Brown, "Online Education."

59. Ibid.

60. Ibid.

61. Ibid.

62. Amanda Hurlbut, "Online v. Traditional Learning in Teacher Education: A Comparison of Student Progress," *American Journal of Distance Education* 32, no. 4 (October 2018): 248–66.

63. Deepak Reddy, "Will Online Education Replace Classroom Education Anytime Soon?" *Forbes*, May 8, 2018, https://www.forbes.com.

64. Ibid.

Chapter Five

Attracting and Retaining Teachers

> Burnout is a real issue, for both first-year teachers and thirty-year veterans. Schools are losing valuable educators, and student achievement is suffering. That's the bad news. The good news is that there are treatments available to immunize new teachers from experiencing the detrimental side effects of burnout, and there are treatments to provide school-wide antidotes.[1]

The first thing that new teachers will most likely have to guard against is being swallowed up by programs and administrative expectations placed upon them. All teachers face both the expectations of new program adjustments as well as the academic progress and achievement of their students. Nevertheless, new teachers must resist the temptation to perform expertly and become involved in school functions at levels that mimic teachers of many years' experience.

Behind each great teacher is someone who took the time to impart the values and wisdom learned through the avenues of experience. It is with this spirit and with this exhortation that veteran educators should hearken back to their first years in their classrooms. Veterans of the classrooms would do well to be reminded that mentoring people to success is what the purpose of building relationships in teaching is all about. They would also do well to reflect on their colleagues that stepped forward to assist them as well.

Any discussion that introduces the development of relationships among educators is inevitably linked to aspects of mentoring and collaboration. For example, it is true that classroom teachers do not desire relationships with programs. Relationships are about people. Still, those new to teaching will have to discover the balance between programs and people.

Those untrained in the traditional sense, and entering the classroom from an environment outside of education, will require extra attention. This group of new teachers will have it doubly difficult in the beginning. There is the likelihood that retaining these teachers may come at a great cost, financially, interpersonally, and to the consistency of a school's academic program.

VALUE OF COLLABORATION

Programs that diminish any authority of teachers, or restrict teachers from providing the best environment for all learners, are already set up to disappoint. Not all teachers that assume classrooms in the nation have adequate training in psychology, human behaviors, and student motivation. Some teachers are fraught with concern over classroom management and discipline strategies, while others are a bit more resolved in this area.

Not all teachers today have come out of traditional teacher education programs. Every teacher who has is going to have to remember this throughout the year. Accordingly, this is where new teacher collaborative work with mentors is so very important and why developing professional relationships can lead to success over time.

Mentoring new teachers and building relationships takes time. One particular reason these relationships are so very important lies in the reality that teachers are thrust into this new age of equity-driven policies and intervention programs—all of which appear outside typical curriculum and standards. The challenges are real.

Teachers today will have to spend more time during each day on behavior issues and in-class remedies of certain behaviors. This, along with teaching from an embedded social justice foundation, where public education has found itself in the twenty-first century.[2] It is imperative that new teachers are helped to get on board with these specifics as quickly as possible and to learn how best to apply the steps and tiers associated with each.

In terms of securing and retaining teachers, those with consistently relational mentors are more likely to grasp the everyday issues more readily. Research indicates that collaboratively mentored teachers are less likely to leave the classrooms and that working together with a trusted mentor has significantly better outcomes. If teacher career longevity is important to school districts, then *collaborative mentoring* should be a significant part of the plan.

Collaborative Mentoring

Many professions use some form of mentoring as they build teams. Some refer to it as *interning*; others, *leading* or *teaming*; and still others, *making disciples*. The principles culled from various professions, pertaining to mentoring, provide a glimpse into what the best mentors do.[3] Building people is the goal of collaborative mentoring.

Anthony Tjan writes that the best mentors focus primarily on three things, in terms of the development of long-term professional relationships that are intercollegial "between mentor and mentee."[4] First, without an effective, long-term collaborative relationship, the data show there are few differences in the decision-making and the teaching between those with mentors and those without.[5] The main difference is in the trusting and transparent relationship between the mentor and the mentee. As they work together, more trust is developed and, accordingly, both then choose to work toward a common goal.

Second, the developing relationship should focus on the character that emerges through the relationship. There should be aspects of oneness that result from mentoring. The development of personal and professional character is even more important than competencies.

Mentors help their mentees jointly by "focusing on helping to shape . . . characters, values, awareness, empathy, and capacity for respect."[6] This focus is highly desired in businesses, as employers are seeking what are called *uniquely human skills*. These skills are what are known by their sister term, *soft skills*.

Soft skills are as essential for teachers as their content knowledge. Mentors can help mentees to build on both sets of these skills and both motivate and hold them accountable for growth.[7] Taken together with character-focused soft skills, and hard skills, this platform sets a new teacher on the path toward career longevity.

Third, a professional mentor must be more loyal to the mentee as a person than he or she would be to an organization, or a business entity.[8] If people are more important than things, then the working relationship between the pair is most important. This is another important aspect of the collaborative oneness developed between mentor and mentee and is key to retaining teachers. Likewise, what is produced in the long run may reveal exponential relational and personal benefits that will later affect academic outcomes for students.

INDUCTION PROGRAMS FOR ALL

There have been studies performed that lead to similar conclusions regarding teacher attrition. These studies seem to point to the idea that challenges faced by teachers in their first few years of teaching are behind many of the reasons teachers leave the classrooms.[9] While it is true that teacher attrition is a major problem for many states, these states are making efforts to resolve their staffing issues.

As a result, states have commissioned studies to find the reasons or causes, and to determine whether attrition can be reversed by improved teacher induction programs. One such state was California.

The California County Superintendents Educational Service Association (CCSESA), in partnership with Hanover Research, has compiled what they have determined as the best practices for teacher induction. Also included is research on administrator induction and mentoring. The implication is that administrators come from a pool of teachers. The less teachers there are, the smaller the pool of teachers aspiring one day to become administrators. However, make no mistake about it. Induction and mentoring are not just for new teachers.

The CCSESA report includes research from states including "Ohio, North Carolina, Illinois, New Jersey, and New York."[10] Two of the key findings of the study are significant and validate both induction and mentoring. These findings include "(1) induction programs have a positive impact on retention and student outcomes; and (2) mentoring plays a key role in effective induction programs for teachers and administrators."[11]

This is good news for those concerned about teacher retention. There is no secret among educators that since the 1990s, the majority of states have required all new teachers to participate in tailored induction programs and had often been assigned mentors for two to three years,[12] depending on the state. Researchers went even further and drew encouraging conclusions, as a result of meta-analyses.

Richard Ingersoll and Michael Strong published a landmark meta-analysis of nearly three decades of teacher induction research and found that even dissimilar state induction programs "have a consistently positive impact in three areas."[13] The areas of positive impact include "(1) teacher retention, (2) classroom instructional practices, and (3) student achievement."[14]

However, the positive impacts are not necessarily long lived, or *reliably* consistent, especially in areas of the inner cities, or areas that are highly impoverished. Teacher turnover is the highest in these areas. It is second highest in remote, rural areas. It seems that *teacher flight* from the inner city and from rural areas has become extremely problematic. This is due in part to the benefits of living and working in the inner cities being often outweighed by the costs.

According to Ingersoll and Strong, "One explanation for the inconsistent findings regarding teacher retention is that although induction could, after a couple of years, positively affect teachers' practices and student achievement in high-poverty, urban public schools, nevertheless, receiving comprehensive induction as opposed to the prevailing induction alone may not be able to persuade teachers to stay in such schools at significantly higher rates."[15]

New teachers should be included in orientation, whether "formal or informal,"[16] where the teachers are introduced to the procedures of the school and how these function for faculty and students. Next, all newly hired teachers should be assigned a direct mentor that will meet consistently in support of the newer teacher. This mentor should be one of veteran status and have been at the school for a period of time to understand the nuances of the specific school and education, in general.

Third, new teachers have greater chances of success in combining orientation and mentoring with continuing professional development. One of the more successful groupings that have proven beneficial when functioning correctly is professional learning communities (PLCs).[17] Relationships between teachers, combined with strategic professional development, show promise in reducing teacher attrition.[18] Collaborative relationships that focus on trust and the development of skill sets are more likely to lead to career longevity.

STAGES OF MENTORING

In this new age of twenty-first-century teacher shortages, the word *mentoring* has taken on new meanings. In the past, there was a certain top-down responsibility incumbent upon veteran teachers personally to assist in the establishment of new teachers in their careers. Vestiges of this philosophy and practice still exist.

Certainly there is a natural confidence and often a high level of respect on the parts of newer teachers who are placed with career teachers. However, a concern today is that with many older teachers retiring and with a number of younger teachers increasingly leaving, who will mentor the Gen Z teachers coming up?

There may be a raft of *new* teachers mentoring ever *newer* teachers. The newer generation of teachers is more collaborative in many ways and this could be a wonderful change, or it could wind up being disastrous. In any case, it might well be a new mentoring paradigm.

In decades past, students were matriculated into postbaccalaureate teacher education programs. Their "student-teaching" was overseen by a "master-teacher," who sometimes informed the student teacher the class was all his or hers, and then spent weeks in the teachers' lounge, checking in every so often on the teacher-in-training.

That was the old paradigm under which an increasing number of retiring teachers had been trained. The sink-or-swim method for one semester, or a full quarter, is no longer vogue. Now, it is vastly different. People tend to burn out faster. People are also entering teaching from all walks and stages of life, and this reality requires a set of different strategies to be employed.

Since mentoring of new teachers is a critical component to training effective teachers and reducing attrition, the National Foundation for the Improvement of Education, the foundation for the NEA, developed a sequence by which they suggest the mentoring of new teachers. They contend any mentoring best includes joint efforts in building people into professionals.

Along these lines, the NEA suggests that collaborative mentoring should include the following three stages:

Stage 1. Focusing on practical skills and general information about policies and procedures of the school and district.

Stage 2. Building relationships that ultimately begin to positively affect the teacher's skills in teaching and effectiveness of classroom management.

Stage 3. Improving the skills of the teacher by professional development that delves deeper into strategies that can be applied to assist students in greater learning outcomes, and to gain additional knowledge toward assessing the various needs of students.[19]

Teaching Is Relational

Today's students training to be teachers are no longer called *student-teachers*. He or she is referred to as an intern, or a mentee. That implies that one or more people, aside from the teacher-overseer, is watching and advising the "potential teacher" out in the field. Mentoring today, in order to be highly successful, requires experienced people in education to spend quality time in the field, observing, evaluating, and building professional relationships with the mentees. This is an example of collaboration mentoring.

Teacher retention is the result of collaborative attention. Any sense of isolation by newer teachers is just one of the reasons for the rise of the professional learning communities. In the words of the late Rick DuFour, "There is simply no evidence that encouraging each teacher to work in isolation in autonomous classrooms to teach his or her own curriculum according to his or her own idiosyncratic philosophy, vision, and discretion creates a school culture that is beneficial to either students or teachers."[20]

Teachers at school sites are often assigned newer teachers to supervise and to be the go-to person when there are questions. Most teachers can be made or broken by the level of support they receive at their school sites, whether working as an intern or after they are hired by a school district. Everyone in education gets busy. However, success for new teachers, as well as veteran teachers, is predicated on others making the time to support those that need extra relational attention.

Support Is Key

Statistics are quite revealing, and the data indicate the reductions in the numbers of teachers remaining in the classrooms are alarming. The data demonstrates that some of the reductions in the numbers of teachers are tied to the lack of on-campus support. Teachers' breaking points are sometimes unpredictable, but when they occur they become a travesty for all involved.

There is one caveat about retention that is out of the hands of the mentor. A generation that has less commitment to career choices may experience higher attrition regardless of the induction and mentoring. Among today's newer teachers it may be likely that they do not envision their work as a career, or a profession, but as a stopgap until something better comes along.

This might be the internal disposition of some of the newer teachers from the first days of their hire. If this is the case, newer teachers entering the workforce have already decided that teaching had become an experiment with a career choice. From this position, the conclusion drawn is that if one career does not pan out, then others are available. The philosophy behind multidecade career choices has all but died. The reality is that attracting and retaining Gen Z teachers, with longevity in mind, might have to be thought about differently.

THE ROLE OF PROFESSIONAL DEVELOPMENT

The number of noncredentialed and alternatively licensed teachers is rising each year, and various programs have been created in attempts to meet the demand of new teachers. The goal of most of these new programs "is to provide a quicker path into the teaching profession than traditional programs while still providing more preparation than might be required for an emergency credential."[21]

Essentially, alternative programs allow individuals who have already obtained a bachelor's degree "to bypass the time and expense involved in attaining a teaching degree or completing a graduate program."[22] The methods used to gain entry into classroom teaching are changing, and with these changes the role of professional development in connection to mentoring becomes more and more important.

New Teachers' Training

New teachers are expected to come into the job with certain qualifications, and within reason, expectations of expertise come along with them. That is, teachers are expected to know how to teach, or learn quickly how to do so. They must also know their content and decide what is important to teach, manage their classrooms, plan lessons, execute these lessons, and memorize the routines of their classrooms and their schools in timely fashion. If this is asking a lot for any newly trained teacher, then consider the untrained!

Noncredentialed teachers have to not only learn all of the above but also manage living through each day on their jobs. Frequently, new teachers that are products of alternative certification "begin working in the classroom while completing their coursework—sometimes from the very beginning of the program—rather than in the last year of a traditional program. . . . However, while alternative certification programs can offer quicker paths to teaching, in some cases the required coursework and program length are the same as traditional paths."[23]

Other very real aspects of any teaching job are also subject to training. New teachers are often required to be enrolled in a certain number of credential courses as a contingency to keeping their jobs after hire. The fact is that there is great turnover year in and year out, when inexperienced and noncredentialed teachers are asked to maintain the composite pressures of veteran teachers, and attend classes themselves. Many who leave the classroom within the first three years do so by weighing the costs and benefits of the job and decide the expenditure of time, energy, and personal finances are simply not equitable.

Since roughly "20 percent of new teachers are already entering the profession through alternative certification programs,"[24] there is a growing need for additional development for these teachers. This development takes on a greater sense of urgency since many of the alternative programs are "less selective than traditional programs and attract a broader pool of applicants, especially mid-career professionals looking to change their career tracks," which may increase the overall "diversity of the teacher pool."[25]

What Is Practical?

As mentioned earlier, data demonstrate that early intervention in a teacher's career can lead to success for the teacher. Mentoring and providing tangible and practical professional development is essential in feeling part of a team. The research is clear that alternative programs reach several particular demographics and help to fill positions in locations where the need for teachers is most critical.

Consequently, alternative certification programs initially tend to "attract minority and male recruits and these recruits may be more likely to choose to work in urban or high-need schools."[26] However, it has already been established that teachers do not last long in the inner-city schools.

One has to speculate as to whether the cohort method, or district-provided professional development units, could help to reduce the rate of teacher attrition. If the latter is the determination, then the development of a local professional academy—one that would suffice for states and county offices of education—might well be the paradigm of success in this changing world of teacher training and classroom teacher hiring.

For example, local colleges and universities with education majors could assist in the development of an academy that meets both the needs of districts and the basic requirements of the institutions and the state in question. It could be envisioned as an accelerated pathway. The larger difference between this and the typical in-service is that the academy is, at its core, developmental to the teacher's craft and credentials.

In-services are more topical, whereas an academy approach would be more focused on development aspects. To the untrained, an academy as such could be just the right idea to assist with both the success of the new teacher and longevity of his or her career.

THE ROLE OF SCHOOL LEADERSHIP

The issues faced by teachers, certified or not, are highly predictable. Therefore, going forward it is necessary to have an administrator that fully understands each of the struggles contained within the stages of development of new teachers. In a general sense, administrators are the hub of teacher mentoring, and their confidence and assistance can bolster the confidence of all teachers. Conversely, lack of administrative support is a primary reason for teacher attrition.

A good administrator that is supportive will regularly check on the teachers in need, make certain to provide the right close mentors for the teachers, and will insist on practical teacher development modules for building his or her staff. One of the most unfortunate things about school leaders today is the lack of time they actually have to act in accord with the title.

Administrators tend to be forced to be more concerned about avoiding controversies. They often find their days being spent on important but tedious and impersonal tasks. Yet one of the most often repeated statements given by teachers as to why they left their jobs is a lack of administration support. One school principal shared that his main job each day was to avoid a lawsuit. So, he became in his words a "yes person" to all the special interest groups and mediocrity became status quo, in order to be all things to all people and seldom special to few.

Administrators who insulate themselves eventually succumb to the new education culture, which is characterized by bureaucracy and career climbing. The results of this type of lack of administrative support are lower morale on campuses and increases in teacher exits from schools.

In the case of the secondary school administrator seeking to avoid a lawsuit, his faculty began to leave the once-distinguished school. The school quickly became a haven for special needs students, where 504s increased, and a place of intervention programs that isolated teachers from their skill sets as they facilitated student learning and managed their classrooms. Social emotional learning and restorative justice began to be applied to students committing adult-level offenses. Teachers felt unsupported by the ladder-climbing career administrator, as programs engulfed the school.

For the administrator, filling his classrooms with substitute teachers had become more and more challenging as the word spread his school was no longer one of first choice. The reality is that these types of constraints placed on administrators and teachers have secondary effects that may lead to increases in teacher attrition and disintegration of unity. The administrator in question wondered what happened to his award-winning school and stellar group of collaborative teachers. The new culture of education had apparently achieved its goal of mediocrity.

RETHINKING PROFESSIONAL DEVELOPMENT

First, school districts have to convince their teachers that they are the ones who know best and that any professional training they will undertake should be relevant and aligned with the goal of making them better teachers. A more appropriate slant might be to rephrase *professional development* to something more akin to what really takes place. If teaching is a profession, it is unlike any other profession. Consequently, a phrase to apply to the process of building new teachers in-house could be *teacher-craft development*. However, for the sake of nomenclature, the process will be referred to in its traditional form.

The onset of multiple points of access to the classroom through alternative certification may mean that those coming from other professions are the true and trained professionals, just seeking to make a difference in another environment. The possibility of a more diverse, more life-experienced, and older professional cohort may be the next generation of teachers for twenty-first-century classrooms.

In fact, pertinent to this, "research has found no distinction between alternatively and traditionally certified teachers"[27] in terms of their entrance exam scores at college, the selection of college attended and from which they graduated, and the degree attainment. The differences become highly noticeable when they are in front of the classroom.

Second, any teacher development that is offered has to be both informational and practical. The research indicates that new teachers who are subject to professional development, including additional instructional methods training and even classroom management strategies, are more likely to remain on the job.[28] A third consideration that justifies professional development for new teachers is the series of hoops put in place for them to keep their jobs, renew their certifications, and for some to move toward tenure.

Suggested Professional Development

When considering what type of on-site professional development to design for schools with new teachers, whether called an academy or known by another name, several questions must be asked when considering professional development.

1. Are the teachers in need elementary, middle, or secondary? This is important to know, for example, when it comes to methods of discipline and to developing relationships, with students, classroom management, academic content knowledge, and many others. Any professional development should be strategic to grade levels and age appropriate.
2. How much training does a teacher need in psychology and behavior management in dealing with today's emotionally charged and special-needs-challenged classroom environments? Strategies that are tied to a district behavior policy should be the focus.
3. What is the extent of technology use expected by the teachers in the classrooms, as well as the school policies regarding student use? The proliferation of smart devices across the employment horizon should provide easier entry points, interns of technology inclusion for newer teachers.
4. How is a teacher to understand his or her use of social media and balance this with student use of the same during class time? This is a critical area of concern.
5. What is the extent of classroom discipline training and training in intervention strategies? How do these apply in real-world settings?
6. What levels of relationships and collaboration are expected by the teachers with fellow faculty, students, and parents, and how are these relationships managed and mentored?

One can see that taking college classes to fulfill credit and course requirements may not meet the needs that new teachers have when signing on to teach—especially those from nontraditional programs. Boards of education that empower districts to innovate their own teacher development in-house are serving immediate needs and might well reduce the rate of attrition. Such innovations cannot hurt. But bear in mind, there is no secret sauce.

In this modern era, financial and personal investments in teachers, their training, and essentially their lives can no longer be left only to teacher training institutions. Districts must consider changing their mindsets toward more practical professional development and incorporate more strategic offerings if they are serious about hiring and retaining teachers.

PINNING DOWN THE PROFESSIONAL

This section of the chapter is open to debate. How does one come to admit that where he or she spent nearly four decades of employment has caused deep chasms in conviction because teaching did not turn out to be what was expected. Teachers that have parents and friends in true professions often do not understand the very things that are taken for granted.

Once they visit schools, or leave their current employment to pursue a career in teaching, they find out exactly why teaching is different. Teaching can be a career, but it cannot be defined as a normal profession. Included in the following are multiple observations helping to draw this conclusion. [29]

Those considering teaching to be a profession should pause to reflect on whether teaching bears any comparative resemblance to the professions of others.

- Professionals can take coffee breaks.
- Professionals can avoid standing out in the cold waiting for students.
- Professionals are not issued whistles for recess duties.
- Professionals can spend thirty minutes in impromptu chats with colleagues.
- Professionals go out to lunch for an hour and often can count it as work related.
- Professionals can often complete paperwork or digital records and other job-related tasks within office workers during a given workday.
- Professionals can often sit down occasionally in quiet reflection.
- Professionals can often have a secretary take messages or hold all calls.
- Professionals can fire inept workers, or be fired themselves for the same.
- Professionals are not at risk of being hit, spit at, or bitten by their clients.
- Professionals do not have to put up with being sworn at, screamed at, and verbally abused at work and online.
- Professionals are not held to a standard of their patients' or clients' outcomes on assessments.
- Professionals do not expend excessive energy to convince and motivate the unmotivated to behave and learn because employment depends on this success.

Teaching Is More a Blue-Collar Trade

Teaching is not a profession in the strict definition of the term. Teaching is a blue-collar trade with special triage training for student needs that have little to do with teaching. This is especially true at the elementary levels. Schools are social agencies today with a variety of social workers assuming professional credentialed or licensed specialist roles. Education is actually more a profession.

One of the major reasons that teaching can be described as a trade is that teaching has apprenticeships modeling, in terms of learning what and how to do things. This is reminiscent of the types of standards and practices of standards that are often found in union work. Trades do things certain ways, and such is the case with developing lesson plans, instructional strategies, and methods of assessment.

Like all other trades, teachers can belong to a labor union and are limited by a contract and state and federal laws. They must comply with these policies and laws to earn and/or maintain a credential. In states that are right-to-work states, the pay is lower and the benefits are sometimes fewer.

Many teachers would be challenged to name a "profession" that is in such great demand and always will be but pays so little. Others would be hard-pressed to realize the myriad "nonprofessional" roles associated with being a teacher. The fact is that professionals are not good at being all things to all people. They are good at what their exclusive training certifies. The fact that teachers have so many hats to wear is more than an implication as to the nature and title of their jobs.

DEFINING THE TWENTY-FIRST CENTURY TEACHER

The mindset of today's teachers is very different than mindsets of previous generations of teachers. At the elementary level (K–6), the list of roles assumed by teachers sounds less like instruction and more like counseling facilitation and behavioral psychology, but without the credentials.

Since more teachers are reaching into the emotions of children, with the hope that they will somehow begin to parlay that learning into behavioral changes, there needs to be an understanding of social emotional learning (SEL) at the outset. SEL is making inroads into schools all over the nation. Teachers are finding they are having to sacrifice academic teaching time to focus on social and emotional skills for children.

A recent survey was taken of about 1 percent of the California Teachers Association membership, which equates to about 3,500 survey respondents. Those surveyed included nurses, psychologists, and counselors. Forty percent of the respondents indicated they had little to no training in alternative discipline approaches. The age of teacher shortages will find more and more teachers placed into classrooms without some of the necessary skills and basic training in classroom management.[30] At the same time, fewer teachers mean fewer mentors.

Social-Emotional Learning

The intention with SEL is that it should translate into the lives of students and provide a framework to enhance their learning. Teachers today are required to spend more time in preparing students to act more empathetic and more socially responsible with their choices and behaviors. Some subjects at the elementary level have to be sacrificed because of the choice to spend more time integrating SEL into teaching, as well as in other nonacademic programs.

Advocates of SEL argue that the program should be embedded in all that is taught at school, and not taught as a stand-alone program. If this was to occur, it would require an overhaul of some curriculum. It has been said before and it is worth saying again: teachers want to teach.

Certainly, what attracts almost every teacher into teaching is the opportunity to educate children. However, much more of what is done today in schools is based on *needs*, the likes of which are outside the skill sets of most trained teachers. If schools are serious about needs-based education and a comprehensive SEL framework embedded in all that takes place at schools, then is this not one of the better reasons for a quality on-site professional development academy? Consider the following roles that teachers assume without having the requisite training that coincides with the roles.

The following list is a nonexhaustive set of roles assumed by most modern teachers, particularly elementary school teachers. Any number of these roles are played out on any given day. Sadly, some traditional teacher training programs, and others offering alternative pathways to certification, do not adequately prepare their teachers for many of these roles. Consequently, many roles have to be learned on the job.

- Counselor
- Communicator
- Referee
- Curriculum differentiator
- Behavior moderator
- Special needs facilitator
- Classroom tutor
- Student data manager
- Special needs accommodator
- Relationship cultivator and nurturer
- Negotiator and problem solver
- Purveyor of empathy and emotion
- Grower of mind-sets
- Classroom manager and disciplinarian
- Writer and planner

- Corrector
- Comedian
- Proficient in social-emotional learning
- Parent liaison
- Bus duty officer
- Explainer of neuroscience and stages of student brain development
- Manager of helicopter, lawnmower, and bulldozer parents[31]

DRIVERS OF TEACHER ATTRITION

Along with the surprises that come with a number of roles associated with today's classroom teachers, what else could be a factor that might cause teachers to wonder what exactly they had gotten themselves into? One of the answers to this question is the inordinate amount of time spent teaching to one test or another.

In twenty-first-century American schools, the emphasis on teaching is not based on virtues that promote life skills, lifelong learning, and the taking of responsibility that will help children as they grow into adults. Rather, "the emphasis is on ensuring each child scores above a certain percentage on tests."[32] The drivers of attrition are unmistakable signposts on the education superhighway,[33] and testing is a neon sign along this pathway.

WHICH HAT TO WEAR?

Teachers are required to wear many hats, in addition to their instructional headwear, in order to maximize the opportunities for students to successfully pass their assessments. Along with motivating students, there is the required teaching of mathematics, English, literature, and other subjects that are assessed. In the midst of this, teachers are supposed to be equity-minded and seek out opportunities to point out and correct bias and actively promote diversity at all grade levels.

Bryan Steinberg, former secondary history teacher, is "one of the many teachers and other public education workers who have quit their profession and moved on completely."[34] Steinberg notes that among all of the other elements teachers must now focus on in classrooms, such as assessments, building student self-esteem, and various learning opportunities, the teachers' workload is unrealistic. He states, "I guess 'the first thing was money, among other things . . . we had a contract that was canceled, and I wasn't given my promised pay raise for five years. . . . We work 60 hours a week, and we are only paid for 37–38 hours per week.'"[35]

Statistics appear to verify Steinberg's comments. Focusing on racial issues, assessments, SEL, and a bevy of other important elements in school is reshaping schools into less and less of the academic institutions Americans need in order to be competitive with other nations.

The extent to which this reshaping is felt can be construed by the numbers. In "the first 10 months of 2018, public educators quit at the average rate of 83 per 10,000 on staff. It's the highest rate of public education departures since records began in 2001."[36]

Schools have become satellites for a host of issues and seem less focused on academics. Teachers understand they are social agents, at times. Yet when social agentry begins to usurp academics, social agentry becomes a social agency.

The pressures on teachers are great. Teachers are expected to act as parents, counselors, disciplinarians, tutors, and more. They have to create lesson plans, grade papers, coach, mentor, sponsor clubs, attend meetings, communicate with parents, and then when there is time, they have their teaching. Science and social studies are often a combined compromise, relegated to once a week. Classroom sizes range from fifteen to thirty students. If only five of those have mental health problems, that is a huge burden for the teacher.[37] Teachers are not trained as mental health experts.

Add these to the pressure to secure a passing score on state tests or national standardized assessments. Teachers must accomplish all of this while maintaining their own wellness. Through all of this, repeated daily and weekly, teachers may very well develop "their own mental health issues to overcome each day."[38] One can only wonder at what point teachers say they have had enough.

More Data

In 2016, teachers and school officials from districts all over the state of California participated in an online survey, conducted by the California Teachers Association (CTA). The survey revealed teacher frustrations, many of which were expected, in the face of the rollout of new behavioral programs across the state. Some teachers were trained in intervention programs, and others were trained in behavior modification programs. Teachers used one or the other and found some success.

Other teachers found neither of them worked to any effective degree of behavioral correction. One additional group of teachers in the survey petitioned for training in something that would assist them in managing their classrooms in general. Increasing the amount of quality professional development can help to reduce frustrations. But the professional development cannot be treated as another item added to the already-full plates of teachers.

When it comes to mentoring and classroom management, a one-size-fits-all program will not work in all classrooms. Different cultures, races, and ethnicities come from backgrounds that need to be understood. A good teacher needs to be culturally relevant to his or her students. A good mentor can help to fill in some of the details on how to relate to students of various backgrounds and assist in helping new teachers to learn the core aspects of managing people within and across their differences.

BUILDING EFFECTIVE RELATIONSHIPS

What does it take to build effective and empathetic relationships with colleagues and students? First, it takes an understanding of people. Understanding people means knowing how they think, how they learn, and the methods of compromise necessary to arrive at cooperative and collegial understanding. Also, there must be a keen awareness of self, a solid understanding of the dynamics of externals, such as extended families, as well as the personalities of the people that comprise these families. Building effective relationships comes with certain built-in costs and benefits. In addition, good relationships also grow from a decent dose of humility.

On the one hand teachers desire to be relational and nurturing. On the other hand, laws and policies work against this fundamental reality that classroom teaching is primarily about relationships. This places teachers in precarious positions. As the percentages of untrained and/or alternatively certified classroom teachers increase over the next few years, risks that are associated with the percentage increases will be elevated.

In many cases the uses of smart technology elevates the risks. Mentors can save a teacher's career by being there at critical moments and reminding teachers assigned to them to continue to be diligent about making good choices, and the benefits of these choices, as well as the consequences for poor choices. But then, what happens when a mentor goes awry?

Who's Mentoring the Mentors?

The number of veteran teachers either being placed on administrative leave for something inappropriate or being arrested for inappropriate relationships with students is astounding. Some of these teachers served as mentors to other teachers. This begs the question, *who is mentoring the mentors?*

The time has come for states to require schools to train teachers *what is* and *what is not* appropriate in relationships with students and parents. Districts have accomplished this with policies regarding touching and mandatory reporter requirements. So, why not with something just as serious?

For example, teachers should grapple with such questions as follows: (1) Should teachers date the parents of their students? (2) Given technology today, how do teachers balance their personal lives with their public persona as teachers? A good teacher mentor can help to bring clarity to many gray areas in today's classroom teaching, unless the good mentor sacrifices his or her reputation for the pursuit of a secret self.

The case of Emily Salazar of Frontier High School in Bakersfield, California, is a prime example of what happens to a mentor-teacher when one's private life meets up with one's public life. Salazar was discovered having made multiple adult films for a pornography website that both she and her husband moderated. Salazar's husband did all of the filming of the group sex scenes for the high school "professional." The mentor-teacher became a viral distraction for thousands of people in schools and across the entire district's education community.

An obvious question asked in circumstances like these should be whether what is done on one's own time affects the job a teacher and mentor has to perform. In seeking to answer with her reputation in mind, the major question to consider should be whether her private behavior and secret lifestyle personally affected the relationships with her own family, her church, students and their parents, colleagues, and the larger community.[39]

Although no laws were broken, and Salazar has since resigned, teachers must always remember they are expected to live above reproach as public figures. Not many would disagree it is fair to be held to such a standard. Salazar no doubt was good at her job as teacher-mentor. However, the consequences of her actions in private spilled over in the public domain.

The building of relationships takes a while, but the destruction of them can be completed in one bad choice. The belief that they do not need to be held to a higher standard reduces the need for mentors to instruct teachers about the importance of the title of teacher. Could this be a major reason some teachers find themselves in trouble and wonder why?

Mentors representing induction programs should be asking the difficult questions of new teachers during orientation. They can begin with the following query: do today's teachers even know the out-of-class impact they have on the psyches of the communities in which they work? Maybe mentors should be asking themselves this key question.

Mentoring Parents

It may be difficult to read, but some teachers are bullied by parents and decide that teaching is not their career choice after all. Every teacher probably knows a parent that fits somewhere between the oft-repeated two categories of parents: helicopter and lawnmower. Aside from hovering and clearing pathways for their children, there are parents who take their involvement to new depths. These are the bulldozer parents.

Along with the parents that contest most everything about their child's schooling, bulldozer parents plow through any and all circumstances.[40] The motivation for these types of parents is to move heaven and earth on behalf of their children, plowing new paths, by either forceful action or strategic undermining and manipulation.

Aggressive types of parents "can be challenging to work with."[41] Yet these parents can also be some of the school's greatest assets. As a result, it is in the overall best interest of the students in the classroom and the teacher to develop a collaborative working relationship with these types of parents. Simply put, find ways to use their energies and become involved.

Despite the negative connotation, aggressive parents do not let obstacles stand in their way of progress. They find ways to get things done, usually if there is a benefit to their child or children. They are problem solvers, and teachers should never avoid providing opportunities for all types of parents to work their skills and their charms to the advantage of their classrooms.

For example, the most challenging parents are often the "organizers of potlucks, the raisers of funds, the school board petitioners, the supporters of teachers, and so much more. . . . So how do we work with parents who don't want their kids to face consequences?"[42] The short answer is to get them involved so that their involvement is of great benefit to all students in their own child's classroom.

Focusing on deepening relationships should be the key. Sometimes this means swallowing pride and examining one's heart, and focusing on the positive. Mentoring parents is just as significant toward classroom success and teaching children and mentoring teachers. Is this out of the realm of the job as teacher? No, not today. To illustrate, administrator Trevor Muir points out ways for teachers to build successful relationships with their students' parents.

First, he encourages teachers to diffuse situations with third-party stories that do not involve the student-in-question. Second, he asks educators to work hard to become partners with the parents over the issues that need to be solved and find solutions. This is often done best by lifting up students so that parents understand there are issues that need to be addressed, and not his or her child, as a person.[43]

Third, a strategy not mentioned by Muir is to make it a point to communicate with the student when he or she returns to school, and make it known that the relationship between teacher and student is solid and moving forward.[44] However, even after all of this is accomplished, things "come down to a standard set for your school. Sometimes growth only happens when students struggle, and there might be parents unwilling to accept that. Those are times when the school leader has to realize they might not ever get to be friends with everyone, and that is okay."[45] Mentoring parents has become a very important role for today's teachers. They are, after all, the parents of our shared students.

Mentoring Students

Although "building relationships with students isn't always simple,"[46] there is no short supply of suggestions as to the best ways to accomplish the development of these relationships. In today's education world, every teacher should see his or her work as that of more than teacher. Each is a mentor.

Paula Denton explains, "The more we know about the child the more we can build learning environments and curriculums that are going to work for them."[47] This is sound advice. The words of a teacher "can create an atmosphere of curiosity, engagement, and respectful interactions, which in turn can shape students' relationships with each other and with their learning."[48] Such is the essence of teachers *mentoring students in relational ways.*

Teacher language is critical not only toward the development of relationships with students but also for the overall atmosphere of student success in the classroom. Denton explains, "Skillful teacher language . . . supports students in three broad ways: gaining academic skills and knowledge, developing self-control, and building their sense of community. Across all of these areas, language is a tool that helps teachers articulate a vision, convey faith that students can attain it, give feedback that names students' strengths, and offer guidance that extends students' skills."[49] *Mentoring students relationally means to be focused on guidance.*

Denton also believes that far too many schools treat relationships with students as if they are a luxury to attain. Frankly, relationships with students are often the reasons teachers come to work each day. She stipulates that building relationships is a necessity and that without them student "learning is lessened."[50]

However, in the development of these relationships, "a distinction should be made . . . between building a 'working relationship' and authentic relationship with students."[51] Teachers must never cross the line and participate in an inappropriate relationship with students.[52]

Mentoring students is highly relational and should be approached with caution. The reason for the caution is due to the possibilities of misunderstanding of the attention given. Again, relationships are built over time, but they can be destroyed in less than sixty seconds.

Positive Action Steps

The tips offered by education researchers can be overwhelming at times. There is no one model or formula for establishing relationships with students. However, there are some positive steps that can be taken to move in the direction of beneficial and positive relationships between teacher and students.

To begin, "if you are able to authenticate that 'working relationship' with genuine interest and personalization, more human and affectionate terms for the relationship can grow, resulting in the often-elusive 'student engagement' while also making your job—and life—easier, and your classroom a more enjoyable place for everyone to be."[53] What teacher would not desire a more enjoyable work environment?

Positive steps are action steps taken by teachers toward students. When developing relationships with students, teachers are actually mentoring. The more steps a teacher takes toward developing relationships in classrooms with students, the more one comes to understand that teachers are actually jacks-of-all-trades, basic generalists making efforts to demonstrate some level of proficiency, as well as realize interpersonal successes for any given day.

CONCLUSION

In closing out this chapter on mentoring, there is provided a list of several practical elements that teachers should consider as they mentor students relationally.[54]

- Teachers should provide support of every kind. This includes academic, emotional, and psychological support.
- Teachers can become quite popular by practicing the Golden Rule consistently.
- Teachers would do well to call home for students' good behavior more often than students' bad behavior.
- Teachers should treat all students as individuals. They can accomplish this by making certain to discover what interests them.
- Teachers must avoid sarcasm and sarcastic comments that diminish students' self-esteem and confidence.
- Teachers must avoid setting up favorite students over other students.
- Teachers must be under control and be cautious never to lose their tempers.
- Teachers must be fair and consistent in meting out classroom discipline and student correction.
- Teacher instruction should incorporate problem-based learning and assessments. These problem-based learning opportunities should be applicable to some facets of students' lives in the real world. In this way, the teacher's instruction and the learning can be deemed relational.
- Teachers must be good listeners to demonstrate that they care about their students and their concerns.

Throughout any given year, there are times when teachers and students demonstrate high levels of likeability. Teaching students should never result in favoritism or tend toward any type of popularity contest. That is not mentoring; it's favoring. But "skilled educators know that value of having good relationships with students. Establishing goodwill can help minimize classroom disruptions, improve student engagement, and reduce stress for everyone."[55] New teachers and veterans should remember this always as they seek to build and mentor relationships among teachers, parents, and students.

NOTES

1. Jill Berkowicz, Ann Meyers, and Jennifer Cleary, "Reversing Teacher Burnout Is a Possibility within Reach," *EdWeek*, August 10, 2017, http://blogs.edweek.org.
2. Young Ah Lee, "What Does Teaching for Social Justice Mean to Teacher Candidates?" *Professional Educator* 35, no. 2 (Fall 2011): 1–20, https://files.eric.ed.gov.
3. Anthony K. Tjan, "What the Best Mentors Do," *Harvard Business Review*, February 27, 2017, https://hbr.org.
4. Ibid.
5. Ibid.
6. Ibid.
7. Schaffhauser, "Employers Want."
8. Tjan, "What the Best Mentors Do."
9. Richard M. Ingersoll, "Beginning Teacher Induction: What the Data Tell Us," *Phi Delta Kappan* 93, no. 8 (May 2012): 47–51, https://eric.ed.gov.
10. "Best Practices in Teacher and Administrator Induction Programs," *California County Superintendents Educational Services Association*, June 2016, http://ccsesa.org.
11. Ibid.
12. Ibid.
13. Richard M. Ingersoll and Michael Strong, "The Impact of Induction and Mentoring Programs for Beginning Teachers: A Critical Review of the Research," *Review of Educational Research* 81, no. 2 (April 2011): 201–33, https://www.gse.upenn.edu. Cf. "Best Practices," 3–4.
14. Ingersoll and Strong, "Impact of Induction." Cf. "Best Practices," 4–5.
15. Ibid.
16. "Best Practices," 4–5.
17. Ibid.
18. Harry Wong and Rosemary Wong, "Schools That Beat the Academic Odds," *Teachers Net Gazette*, April 1, 2008, https://www.teachers.net.
19. "Best Practices."
20. Richard DuFour, "The Professional Teacher," All Things PLC, April 18, 2007, http://www.allthingsplc.info.
21. Julie Rowland Woods, "Mitigating Teacher Shortages: Alternative Teaching Certification," *Education Commission of the States*, May 2016, https://www.ecs.org, 2.
22. Ibid.
23. Ibid.
24. Ibid.
25. Ibid.
26. Lorraine Evans, "Job Queues, Certification Status, and the Education Labor Market," *Education Policy* 25, no. 2 (March 22, 2010): 5. Cf. Woods, "Mitigating Teacher Shortages," 3.
27. Woods, "Mitigating Teacher Shortages," 3.
28. Ibid.

29. Ernest J. Zarra III, *The Teacher Exodus: Reversing the Trend and Keeping Teachers in the Classrooms* (Lanham, MD: Rowman & Littlefield, 2018), passim. Cf. Melissa Bowers, "7 Reasons You Might Not Want to Teach Anymore," *Huffington Post*, December 6, 2017, https://www.huffingtonpost.com.

30. Jane Meredith Adams, "Most Teachers in California Say They Need More Training in Alternatives to Suspensions, Survey Finds," *EdSource*, May 7, 2017, https://edsource.org.

31. Duncan Lindsay, "20 Jobs That All Teachers Are Expected to Do but Get No Thanks For," *Metro*, October 10, 2015, https://metro.co.uk.

32. Sarah Morrison, "Why I Quit Teaching: An Insider's Look into the Struggles of Modern Teachers," *Mermaid Traveler Blog*, Bored Teachers, October 6, 2018, https://www.boredteachers.com.

33. Zarra, *Teacher Exodus*, passim.

34. Nicole Vowell, "Teachers Quitting at Highest Rate Ever, Some Leaving Education Completely," *WCPO*, January 4, 2019, https://www.wcpo.com.

35. Ibid.

36. Ibid.

37. "How Teachers Help Students with Mental Health Disorders," *Vantage Point*, 2019, https://vantagepointrecovery.com.

38. Ibid.

39. Jason Kotowski, "Can Frontier High Teacher Who Allegedly Appeared in Porn Videos Keep Her Job? Attorneys Weight In," *Bakersfield Californian*, January 31, 2019, https://www.bakersfield.com.

40. Ernest J. Zarra III, *Helping Parents Understand the Minds and Hearts of Generation Z* (Lanham, MD: Rowman & Littlefield, 2017), passim.

41. Trevor Muir, "Working with Lawnmower Parents," *We Are Teachers*, September 24, 2018, https://schoolleadersnow.weareteachers.com.

42. Ibid.

43. Ibid.

44. Ernest J. Zarra III, *The Entitled Generation: Helping Teachers Teach and Reach the Minds and Hearts of Generation Z* (Lanham, MD: Rowman & Littlefield, 2017).

45. Trevor Muir, "Working with Lawnmower Parents."

46. "32 Tips for Building Better Relationships with Students," *Teach Thought*, April 11, 2018, https://www.teachthought.com.

47. Nina Sears, "Building Relationships with Students," *National Education Association*, accessed May 10, 2019, http://www.nea.org; Cf. Paula Denton and Lynn Bechtel, *The Power of Our Words: Teacher Language That Helps Children Learn*, 2nd ed. (Turners Falls, MA: Center for Responsive Schools, 2015).

48. Denton and Bechtel, *Power of Our Words*, 6.

49. Ibid., 7.

50. Sears, "Building Relationships."

51. "32 Tips."

52. Ernest J. Zarra III, *Teacher-Student Relationships: Crossing into the Emotional, Physical, and Sexual Realms* (Lanham, MD: Rowman & Littlefield, 2013).

53. "32 Tips."

54. Dave Foley, "5 Tips for Better Relationships with Your Students," *National Education Association*, accessed May 10, 2019, http://www.nea.org.

55. Ibid.

Appendix A

*Teacher Vacancies and
Uncertified/Noncredentialed Teachers*

Appendix A

State	Year of data	Minimum number of teachers not fully certified for their teaching assignments	Vacancies left unfilled	Total teachers per state	Comments
Alabama	2015–2016	886	Insufficient data	42,737	291 emergency-certified teachers; 595 alternate-certificated teachers
Alaska	*	*	*	*	Insufficient data
Arizona	2015–2016	1,831	2,476	48,124	More than 4,000 teaching positions were vacant and staffed with underprepared instructors to begin the academic year.
Arkansas	2015–2016	1,184	339	35,430	337 vacancies or long-term substitutes
California	2015–2016	10,209	Insufficient data	267,685	State hired more than 10,000 teachers without full certification, with evidence of more due to other factors, such as out-of-field teachers.
Colorado	*	*	*	*	Insufficient data

Appendix A

State	Year of data	Minimum number of teachers not fully certified for their teaching assignments	Vacancies left unfilled	Total teachers per state	Comments
Connecticut	*	*	*	*	Insufficient data
Delaware	*	*	*	*	Insufficient data
District of Columbia	*	*	*	*	Insufficient data
Florida	2016–2017	0	2,111	180,442	State does not report uncertified teachers.
Georgia	*	*	*	*	Insufficient data
Hawai'i	2015–2016	490	Insufficient data	11,663	382 teachers working without having completed a teacher's education program; 108 additional did not possess a Hawai'i teaching license.
Idaho	2016–2017	920	Insufficient data	15,609	920 on alternate teaching licenses; 78% of school districts reported increasing class size; 64 district requested alternative certification; 37 districts requested provisional authorizations.

State	Year of data	Minimum number of teachers not fully certified for their teaching assignments	Vacancies left unfilled	Total teachers per state	Comments
Illinois	2015–2016	2,700	Insufficient data	132,456	2,700 teachers did not meet requirements for state certification. Background check issues resulted in hundreds of additional school personnel, including some teachers, being ousted in Chicago in 2018.
Indiana	*	*	*	*	Insufficient data
Iowa	2015–2016	0	*	25,684	No teachers were on emergency or provisional licenses. But the state does not report on teacher vacancies.
Kansas	2016–2017	913	*	37,659	One-third of the 913 were on emergency licenses, which are called provisional licenses. In

State	Year of data	Minimum number of teachers not fully certified for their teaching assignments	Vacancies left unfilled	Total teachers per state	Comments
Kentucky	2015–2017	337	*	41,586	2017–2018, there were more than 170 teacher vacancies. The number of teachers on emergency credentials was less than 1%. The state does not report data on uncertified teachers, or whether it increases class size.
Louisiana	*	*	*	*	Insufficient data
Maine	*	*	*	*	Insufficient data
Maryland	2015–2016	661	*	59,194	In 2015–2016, 1.5% were teaching with conditional certificates. Also, 8.9% of courses were taught by teachers categorized as "not highly qualified."

State	Year of data	Minimum number of teachers not fully certified for their teaching assignments	Vacancies left unfilled	Total teachers per state	Comments
Massachusetts	2016–2017	1,874	*	71,859	During the 2016–2017 school year, 2.6% of teachers were not licensed for the assignment they were given to teach.
Michigan	2016–2017	1,136	*	85,038	1,136 teachers were teaching with emergency certification. The state reports only on those with emergency certification.
Minnesota	2015–2016	1,235	*	55,690	1,234 teachers were not licensed but were teaching with special permission. The state has not released data on highly qualified teachers.
Mississippi	2015–2016	109	*	32,311	The state does not count the number of teachers not certified

Appendix A

State	Year of data	Minimum number of teachers not fully certified for their teaching assignments	Vacancies left unfilled	Total teachers per state	Comments
					for their teaching assignments. 5.1% of courses were taught by teachers designated as "not highly qualified."
Missouri	2016–2016	1,159	*	67,356	0.7% of teachers were on temporary teaching certificates. 1% of teachers were teaching with substitute credentials, expired credentials, or no credentials at all. 3.8% of courses in the state were taught by teachers designated as "not highly qualified."
Montana	2015–2016	*	785	10,234	The state reports on teacher vacancies but not on uncertified teachers.

State	Year of data	Minimum number of teachers not fully certified for their teaching assignments	Vacancies left unfilled	Total teachers per state	Comments
Nebraska	2016–2017	206	47	22,988	206 positions in public school districts were not filled by a fully qualified teacher. 4% of the state's districts may have hired uncertified teachers or have unfilled vacancies.
Nevada	2016–2016	560	*	21,656	The state does not report data on various actions taken by districts to mitigate teacher shortages, such as increased class sizes and hiring substitutes.
New Hampshire	*	*	*	*	Insufficient data
New Jersey	2016–2017	4,083	*	115,067	In 2016–2017, the state granted 239 emergency certificates and issued 3,844 certificates of

State	Year of data	Minimum number of teachers not fully certified for their teaching assignments	Vacancies left unfilled	Total teachers per state	Comments
					eligibility. The latter are granted on the basis of either meeting requirement for academic study or passing applicable tests. Certificate of eligibility holders are required to complete a valid teacher education program while teaching.
New Mexico	2016–2017	443	*	*	The state had 443 teacher vacancies, which were later filled by long-term substitutes or uncertified teachers. The state also does not report data on teachers who have "highly qualified teacher" status.

State	Year of data	Minimum number of teachers not fully certified for their teaching assignments	Vacancies left unfilled	Total teachers per state	Comments
New York	2015–2016	14,735	*	203,781	4,210 teachers had no valid teaching certificate. 14,735 teachers were teaching outside of their certification areas.
North Carolina	2015–2016	2,007	*	99,320	In 2015–2016, 2% of teachers were not fully certified. This means they were teaching on lateral entry, alternative, or emergency licenses.
North Dakota	2015–2016	0	*	9,049	In 2015–2016, no courses were taught by teachers on emergency credentials. However, 0.11% of core academic courses were taught by teachers defined as "not highly qualified."

Appendix A

State	Year of data	Minimum number of teachers not fully certified for their teaching assignments	Vacancies left unfilled	Total teachers per state	Comments
Ohio	2016–2017	0	*	106,526	During the 2016–2017 academic year, no courses were taught by teachers on temporary or provisional certification. 1.7% of core academic courses in 2015–2016 were taught by teachers who were not fully certified.
Oklahoma	2016–2017	1,160	*	42,073	1,160 emergency credentials were issued in 2016–2017. The state does not report highly qualified teacher data.
Oregon	2015–2016	832	*	27,850	The state issued 832 provisional licenses, which included emergency, expedited, restricted,

State	Year of data	Minimum number of teachers not fully certified for their teaching assignments	Vacancies left unfilled	Total teachers per state	Comments
Pennsylvania	2015–2016	1,428	*	122,030	conditional, limited, or interim licenses. Full-time positions were filled by teachers with emergency permits. The state does not include teachers who are uncertified for their assignments, such as interns or those teachers designated as "not highly qualified."
Rhode Island	2015–2016	160	*	9,471	160 teachers were on emergency certification in 2015–2016. The state issues emergency certification to individuals who do not qualify for full certification, upon request of the

Appendix A 137

State	Year of data	Minimum number of teachers not fully certified for their teaching assignments	Vacancies left unfilled	Total teachers per state	Comments
					superintendent of schools—but only after the position is advertised statewide. 2% of classes in the state were taught by teachers defined as "not highly qualified."
South Carolina	2015–2016	*	481	49,475	The state reported 481 vacancies in 2015–2016. This data does not include spots filled by underprepared teachers, or those with alternative certifications.
South Dakota	2016–2017	*	69	9,618	At the beginning of the 2016–2017 school year, there were 69 vacancies. The state does not report numbers of uncertified teachers. The state

State	Year of data	Minimum number of teachers not fully certified for their teaching assignments	Vacancies left unfilled	Total teachers per state	Comments
					does offer emergency or provisional licenses. 2.24% of core academic courses were taught by teachers designated "not highly qualified."
Tennessee	2015–2016	40	*	65,341	In 2015–2016, 40 licenses were issued to degreed teachers but who were without valid state teaching licenses. The state did not report highly qualified teacher data.
Texas	2015–2016	22,791	*	342,257	In 2015–2016, 1,478 core academic teachers were teaching on emergency, or nonrenewable, state teaching permits. 14,555 were teaching

Appendix A   139

State	Year of data	Minimum number of teachers not fully certified for their teaching assignments	Vacancies left unfilled	Total teachers per state	Comments
					on probationary certification, while concurrently enrolled in an alternative certification pathway program. 19,988 teachers were assigned outside of the grade level or subject area for which they were assigned. In 2016–2017 data, this number inflated to 21,449.
Utah	2015–2016	148	118	27,374	118 teaching positions were not filled when the 2015–2016 school year started. An additional 148 classrooms were staffed by teachers without full certification. 49 positions were filled by substitutes.

Appendix A

State	Year of data	Minimum number of teachers not fully certified for their teaching assignments	Vacancies left unfilled	Total teachers per state	Comments
Vermont	*	*	*	*	Insufficient data
Virginia	2016–2017	6,626	*	89,968	5% of the teacher workforce in Virginia were teaching on provisional licenses, because they had either not completed or not begun their teacher preparation programs. 6,626 teachers were on provisional licenses.
Washington	2015–2016	3,500	*	59,555	The superintendent of public instruction stated that the annual shortfall of teachers for the state was approximately 3,500.
West Virginia	2016–2017	683	*	20,029	During the school year, 683 positions were filled by a short-term substitute (defined as a vacancy

Appendix A 141

State	Year of data	Minimum number of teachers not fully certified for their teaching assignments	Vacancies left unfilled	Total teachers per state	Comments
					in WV). The state reports only the number of courses taught by long-term and short-term substitutes, and not data on the total number of uncertified teachers.
Wisconsin	2015–2016	1,969	*	58,376	In 2015–2016, the 1,969 emergency licenses issued were more than doubled than those issued in 2013–2014.
Wyoming	2015–2016	76	*	7,615	In 2015–2016, 1% of teachers were teaching on provisional certification. The state does not report on the total number of teachers uncertified for their teaching

State	Year of data	Minimum number of teachers not fully certified for their teaching assignments	Vacancies left unfilled	Total teachers per state	Comments
					assignments. 1.3% of the courses in the state were taught by teachers defined as not highly qualified.

Source: "Uncertified Teachers and Teacher Vacancies by State," Learning Policy Institute, https://learningpolicyinstitute.org.

*According to the Learning Policy Institute, some data was gathered separately from academic years 2015–2016 and 2016–2017. Numbers do not take into consideration the real figures. This is noted for the reader and can be found in the comments section in the following table. Also, the LPI refers to the data as the "minimum number of teachers not fully certified for their teaching assignments" (column 3 of the table), because many states either underestimate or underreport their actual teacher shortage numbers. These underestimates can occur for a variety of reasons, not the least of which are cancelation of courses and classes, increasing of class sizes, and/or starting off the school year with substitute teachers.

Appendix B

Select Sample of State-Level Alternative Pathways to Certification (APCs)

Appendix B

State and BOE link	Statement of APC	Types of alternative pathways for certification	State APC web link
California https://www.ctc.ca.gov/credentials/teach	There are several different alternative pathways a candidate can take to achieve certification in California. These include through a university internship program, a school internship program, teaching at a private school, or the Peace Corps.	• Credentialing through internship • Credentialing through private school experience • Credentialing through the Peace Corps • Transferring teaching licenses from another state • Meeting all testing requirements	https://www.teachercertificationdegrees.com/certification/california-alternative
Florida http://www.fldoe.org	There are several paths to obtaining alternative teacher certification based on the candidate's previous education and experience. Most prospective teachers who majored in a subject other than education will need to complete one of Florida's State-Approved Educator Preparation Programs, which may be offered at a college or university or as an add-on program through select school districts. Many of these programs are designed for those who already hold a bachelor's degree in a subject other than education.	• Temporary teaching certificate • Professional development certification program • Transferring teaching licenses from another state • Meeting all testing requirements	https://www.teachercertificationdegrees.com/certification/florida-alternative

Appendix B   145

State and BOE link	Statement of APC	Types of alternative pathways for certification	State APC web link
Idaho http://sde.idaho.gov/cert-psc/cert	Idaho offers several pathways to alternative teaching licenses. These nontraditional routes are meant to attract experienced professionals who have bachelor's degrees in subjects other than education to the classroom.	• Alternate authorization: content specialist • American Board for Certification of Teacher Excellence • Teach for America • Professional-technical education certification • Meeting all testing requirements	https://www.teachercertificationdegrees.com/certification/idaho-alternative
Massachusetts http://www.doe.mass.edu/licensure/voctech	The typical candidate for the alternative approach to certification has a desire to pursue a career in education and holds a bachelor's degree but lacks the teacher-preparation requirements for an initial certificate. These candidates can follow one of several routes to teacher licensure in Massachusetts.	• Preliminary teaching license • Professional teaching license • Preliminary vocational technical education license • Meeting all testing requirements	https://www.teachercertificationdegrees.com/certification/massachusetts-alternative
Michigan https://www.michigan.gov/mde	The Michigan's Alternate Route to Interim Teaching (MARITC) program is designed to lead to an interim teaching certificate. However, there are other routes that candidates can follow based	• Interim teaching certificate • Occupational certification/authorization for career and technical education • Meeting all testing requirements	https://www.teachercertificationdegrees.com/certification/michigan-alternative

Appendix B

State and BOE link	Statement of APC	Types of alternative pathways for certification	State APC web link
	on previous education and experience.		
New York http://www.highered.nysed.gov/tcert	Alternative teacher preparation programs in New York are joint programs between institutions of higher education and local schools. To be eligible for an alternative preparation program, candidates must have a minimum of a bachelor's degree, which should be in the subject area that the candidate intends to teach. Alternative teacher preparation programs are typically accelerated and lead to the award of either a postgraduate certificate or master's degree depending on the curriculum completed. Completing a master's degree in education can also prepare candidates to teach in New York.	• Transitional A certificate • Transitional B certificate • Transitional C certificate • Professional certificate • Meeting all testing requirements *Additional information pertaining to alternative routes:* • NYC Department of Education Alternative Routes to Certification • New York State Education Department Alternative Teacher Preparation Program • New York State Teacher Certification Examinations • New York State Troops to Teachers Program	https://www.teachercertificationdegrees.com/certification/new-york-alternative
Texas https://tea.texas.gov/Home	In order to qualify for nontraditional teacher certification in Texas, candidates need to possess a bachelor's degree from an accredited institution of higher education. The college or	• Probationary certificate for Texas Alternative certification programs (ACPs) • Career and technical education teacher certification • Highly qualified candidates	https://www.teachercertificationdegrees.com/certification/texas-alternative

State and BOE link	Statement of APC	Types of alternative pathways for certification	State APC web link
	university from which a candidate earned the bachelor's degree must hold accreditation recognized by the Texas Higher Education Coordinating Board. For more information, refer to the agency's List of Recognized Accreditors. Alternative certification programs can commonly be completed in one year as a postgraduate certificate. Teaching candidates also have the option of pursuing a master's degree in education or in a specific subject as part of an approved certification program.	• Meeting all testing requirements	
Washington http://www.k12.wa.us	Alternative routes are designed for career changers and for individuals already working in the school system who want to transition to full-time teaching. Compared to traditional educator preparation programs, alternative routes to a teaching certificate in Washington tend to be shorter, more convenient, more affordable,	• Route 1: For classified instructional employees (e.g., para-educators) with associate's degrees • Route 2: For classified staff with bachelor's degrees • Route 3: For "career changers" with bachelor's degrees • Route 4: For district staff with bachelor's degrees employed	https://www.pesb.wa.gov/workforce-development/growing-future-educators/alternative-routes-to-teacher-certification/alternative-route-descriptions

State and BOE link	Statement of APC	Types of alternative pathways for certification	State APC web link
	and more practically oriented. Enrollment in an alternative route program is through an alternative route provider. Please see the list of providers on their website, and contact a provider for more information.	on conditional or emergency substitute certificate • Meeting all testing requirements	

Index

absentees, 11
addiction. *See* cell phones
adolescence, 5, 6
adolescent choices, 6
adolescents, 5–6
Alabama, 60
Alaska, 61
alternative: certification, 107–108; models, 94, 95–96; pathways to certification, 65–67; Teacher Certification Guide, 93
American: Association of Colleges for Teacher Education (AACTE), 38–39; culture, 45; cactory, 70–71; Institute for Research, 41; Psychiatric Association, 89; University, 17
anxiety, 90
Arizona, 30, 63–64, 68, 69; Department of Education, 63–64
athletics, 21
Atwell, Nancie, 32
authentic : learning, 92, 93; teachers, 92
authority figure, 44

Baby Boomers, 18
Bakersfield, California. *See* Salazar, Emily
Band-Aid approach, 82
bilingual education, 29, 41
beliefs: changing, 3–4
Boise State University, 63
Boland, Ed, 21
Bowers, Melissa, 44

brains: and emotions, 7; and sexuality, 6; developing, 4; neuroimaging, 5; wiring, 5, 90
broken system, 42
Brown v. Board of Education of Topeka, Kansas, 37
Bruno, Bob, 63
building effective relationships, 117; through humility, 117; through nurturing, 117
bulldozers, 45
bullying, 14
bureaucrats, 35, 71
burnout, 105

California, 8, 60, 81, 94, 104; Assembly Committee on Education, 41; County Superintendents Educational Service Association (CSESA), 104; dropouts, 10, 11, 30; Teachers' Association (CTA), 116
Calvert, Laurie, 19
Caucasian, 18, 19
cell phones, 14
Center for Education Data and Research (CEDAR), 93
Christianity, 2
civil discourse, 20
CNN, 32
cognition: cold, 6; hot, 6

collaborative, 34, 102; mentoring, 106; relationships, 105
college rigors, 90
college students: female, 12, 13; male, 12, 13
Colorado, 60
Common Core State Standards, 14, 17, 32, 65, 71
common good, 20
concerns for wellness, 89–90
Connecticut, 60
conservative groups, 37
Council of Chief State School Officers (CCSSO), 86–87
culture: American, 30; broken, 20–21; changes in, 31; of a traditional American, 14; of graduation, 10; of illiteracy, 7, 11; of new education, 14
curriculum, 5

Darling-Hammond, Linda, 28, 33
Davies, John, 90
Davis, Roxanne, 90
declining morale, 35
Deferred Action for Childhood Arrivals (DACA), 15
Delaware, 60
Democratic, 30
Democrats, 19
Denton, Paula, 120
Denver, Colorado, 82
depression, 89
deserving students, 84
DeVos, Betsy, 36
digital technology, 7
discipline policies, 64
Dolores Huerta Foundation, 8
drugs, 14, 20
DuFour, Richard, 106

Eastern religions, 2
economics: career selection, 12; choices, 12
education: as a profession, 29, 77, 80; broken, 19, 20; credentials, 15; degrees in, 13; equity, 21; policy, 16
Educational Testing Service, 56, 87
Educrats, 32
emotional connections, 93

English language development, 29
everyone graduates, 73
Every Student Succeeds Act (ESSA), 11, 34, 42
excellence, 74
expediency: over sufficiency, xv
extreme measures, 82

false: allegations, 91; Finland, 30, 33; Fordham Institute, 37; guilt, 8
flexible moral compass, 2
Florida, 60, 61–62, 88
Frontier High School. *See* Salazar, Emily
future teachers, 91

gender fluidity, 7
generational: change, 2; commonality, 3
Generation Z (Gen Z), 1, 29, 30, 35, 97; brains of, 5; confusion within, 6; entitled, 84; fighting chance, 18; group think, 1, 2, 3, 69, 74; idea promoters, 3; mentoring of, 68; teachers from, 107; troubled students, 9; women of, 31
Global Teacher Prize, 32
Goldhaber, Dan, 93
grading: as evidence of White nationalism, 16; as racial supremacy, 16
in higher education, 16; methods, 16
graduation rates, 71
graduation requirements, 12

Haller, Sonja, 45
Harvard Crimson, 20
Hawaii, 60
Heacock, Sue, 90
higher education, 16
high need schools, 42
high school: graduates, 12; illiteracy, 21; reading levels, 12
hiring, 34
Holdheide, Lynn, 41, 42
Hymowitz, Kay, 21

Idaho, 63
identity, 7, 20
Igwe, Frank, 20
Illinois, 30, 68, 69, 104
inappropriate relationships, 91
inclusion, 20

Indiana, 88
individualism, 20
induction, 34, 35, 56, 103–105
Industrial Revolution, 21
inequality, 18
Ingersoll, Richard, 104
Inoue, Asao B., 17
interning, 102
Iowa, 60

Jesus Movement, 2
Jim Crow, 18
Johnson, Lyndon, 20
Jones, Erika, 36
Journal of American College Health, 90

latent bias, 8
lawnmower parents, 45
leaky bucket syndrome, 30
Learning Policy Institute (LPI), 28, 33, 34, 35, 82
Levin, Jesse, 40
Lewis, C. S., 1
licensure, 34
loan forgiveness, 34, 42
local control funding formula, 42
Lonsdorf, Kat, 30
Lord Acton, 74
Los Angeles, 36
Louisiana, 60
low-performing schools, 42

Machado, Amanda, 9–10
Maine, 60
making disciples, 102
Maryland, 60
Massachusetts, 40, 60, 81
media bias, 14, 20
medical community, 6
mediocrity, 44
mental health therapy, 90
mental illness, 20
mentees, 103
mentoring, 55–56, 57, 58–62, 102; for emerging teachers, 67–68, 69–70; incentives for, 68; of Gen Z teachers, 105; of parent relationships, 118–119; the mentors, 117–118

mentoring students, 120–121; by authentic relationships, 121; by avoiding favoritism, 122; through positive action steps, 120–121
Michigan, 60
Michigan State University, 46
middle class lifestyle, 34
Millennials, 21, 29, 31, 45
Minnesota, 30
minority population, 8
Mississippi, 60
Missouri, 10, 60
moral decline, 14
morale, 35, 64
Moran, Kimberley, 46
Morrison, Sarah, 80
Muir, Trevor, 119
Mulvahill, Elizabeth, 22

Nashville, Tennessee, 68
National Center for Education Statistics, 81
National Council on Teacher Quality, 93
National Education Association (NEA), 14, 15, 105
National Education Association Foundation (NEAF), 70
National Foundation for the Improvement of Education, 105
nationalism, 33
National Public Radio, 30
Netherlands, 5
Network for Transforming Education Preparation (NTEP), 86
neuroscientists, 3, 4
Nevada, 60
New Jersey, 104
new teachers' training, 107
New York, 30, 68, 69, 104
No Child Left Behind (NCLB), 14, 86
noncredentialed teachers, 107
North Carolina, 60, 87, 104
North Carolina Professional Education Preparation Standards Commission, 88
North Dakota, 61
nuclear family, 20, 21

Obama era, 19, 36–37
Ohio, 60, 104

Oklahoma, 30, 40
online teacher education, 96; benefits and costs, 97, 98
Ontario, Canada, 33
Oswalt, Sara, 90

para-fathers, 43
passion, 33, 44, 69
Paul Douglas Teacher Scholarship Program, 94
Pearson, 87, 88
Pekin Community High School, 68
personal bias, 92
Petrilli, Michael, 37
Pink Floyd, 73
pipelines to prison, 8
Plessy v. Ferguson, 37
polarized nation, 16, 18
politicians, 14
politics, 20
pornography. *See* Salazar, Emily
Positive Behavioral Interventions and Support (PBIS), 9
poverty line, 43, 82
Pratt, Rick, 41, 42
Praxis, 56–58, 87
predictions for the future, 81
professional development, 46, 107, 110; district and board rules, 111; questions to consider, 110–111; teacher-craft development, 110
professionalism, 77–79, 112
professional learning communities, 105
psychologists, 43
public education, 15

Race to the Top (RTTT), 14
racial: identity, 9; targeting, 9
racism, white, 17, 18
racist, 56
Real Teachers Talk, 83–84
Reddy, Deepak, 98
Restorative Justice (RJ), 8, 12, 64–65
retaining teachers, 88–89, 102
Rhode Island, 60
Rochester, New York, 68
Roe v. Wade, 7
role of school leadership, 109–110; support, 109; teacher development, 109

Salazar, Emily, 118
same sex marriage, 7
Schneider, Jack, 20
school attendance: Detroit, 11; Washington, D.C., 11
school choice, 19; charter, 15; private, 15
sexuality: and brain development, 6; and personal identity, 7
Shields, Patrick, 40
shifting expectations, 52
Singapore, 30, 33
smart devices, 54; affecting moods, 3; motivate, 3
social: activists, 35; media, 14, 65
social and emotional issues, 14
social-emotional learning (SEL), 21, 113–118
Socialism, 71
social promotions, 73
sociologists, 43
soft bigotry, 17
soft skills, 103
Southern Regional Education Board, 55, 59–60
Spanish, 41
Spiegler, Jinnie, 92
standardized assessments, 15
state certifications, 66–67; general categories, 66; pathway variations, 66–67
states getting serious, 86
states taking measures to reduce requirements, 86–87
STEAM, xiii, 13, 42
Steinberg, Bryan, 115–116
STEM, 31
stop-gap measures, 30
Strong, Michael, 104
students : and absenteeism, 15; and development, 4; and special education, 16, 42; and special needs, 16; of color, 29; that are undocumented, 15
student teacher, 105
surrogate families, 42
Sutcher, Leib, 41

teacher: activists, 21; advocates, 21; anxiety, 15; attrition, 15, 59, 115; authority undermined, 15; burnout, 15,

101; culturally relevant, 116; depression, 15; education, 13; emotional disorders, 15; flight, 104; greatness, 85; illnesses, 15; incentives, 13; injuries, 15; licensure, 30; loan forgiveness, 94; mental health, 15; planning, 80; Preparation Analytics, 86; recruitment, 65–66; retention, 72; salaries, 34, 42; shortages and solutions, 29, 86; strategies, 93; teaming, 102

Teacher Education Assistance for College and Higher Education Grant Program, 94

teachers: accused, 9, 37; as blue collar workers, 112–113; as warm bodies, 30; autonomy, 10; competition for, 72; demand for, 14, 71; in California, 40, 41, 42; middle school, 45; near poverty, 72; roles, 114, 115, 116; secondary, 45; twenty-first century, 113; untrained, 15, 85; walking away, 9

Teach For America (TFA), 39, 62–63, 95

Teach Plus, 87

technology, 15

Tennessee, 60, 69

Texas, 10

Tjan, Anthony, 103

toxicity, 9

trends, 38, 54, 82; wellness, 68

trigger, 18

Tustin, Rachel, 53

UCLA, 38

unions, 72

University of Texas, San Antonio, 90

US Department of Education, 10, 11, 27, 38, 54

Utah, 60

Vail, Arizona, 68

Varkey Foundation, 32

Vermont, 60

violence by students, 14, 20

Virginia, 30, 69

Voke, Heather, 28

Walker, Tim, 46

Walsh, Kate, 93

Watson, Angela, 53

We Are Teachers, 22

Westervelt, Eric, 30, 32

white blindness, 18

white language supremacy, 17

Wisconsin, 60

woke, 7

Wong, Harry, 69

About the Author

Ernest J. Zarra III, PhD, is assistant professor of teacher education at Lewis-Clark State College. Zarra has five earned degrees and holds a PhD from the University of Southern California in teaching and learning theory, with cognates in psychology and technology. He is a former Christian College First Team All-American soccer player, former teacher of the year for a prestigious California public school, and was awarded the top student in graduate education from the California State University at Bakersfield, California.

Zarra has authored nine books, including the following Rowman & Littlefield titles:

The Age of Teacher Shortages: Reasons, Responsibilities, Reactions (2019)

Assaulted: Violence in Schools and What Needs to Be Done (2018)

The Teacher Exodus: Reversing the Trend and Keeping Teachers in the Classrooms (2018)

The Entitled Generation: Helping Teachers Teach and Reach the Minds and Hearts of Generation Z (2017)

Helping Parents Understand the Minds and Hearts of Generation Z (2017)

Common Sense Education: From Common Core to ESSA and Beyond (2016)

The Wrong Direction for Today's School: The Impact of Common Core on American Education (2015)

Teacher-Student Relationships: Crossing into the Emotional, Physical, and Sexual Realms (2013)

Zarra has written more than a dozen journal articles and has designed professional development programs; he is a national conference presenter, a former district professional development leader, former adjunct university instructor, and a member of several national honor societies. He also participates as a presenter in the Lewis-Clark Presents program, bringing special topics to high school students. Originally from New Jersey, he and his wife Suzi, a retired California public school teacher, live in Washington State and enjoy spending time with family, which includes their first grandchild.

www.ingramcontent.com/pod-product-compliance
Lightning Source LLC
Chambersburg PA
CBHW030139240426
43672CB00005B/192

9781475850055